THE
PIRATE
CODE

THE PIRATE CODE

FROM HONORABLE THIEVES TO MODERN-DAY VILLAINS

BRENDA RALPH LEWIS

The Lyons Press

Guilford, Connecticut
An imprint of The Globe Pequot Press

To buy books in quantity for corporate use
or incentives, call **(800) 962–0973**
or e-mail **premiums@GlobePequot.com.**

10 9 8 7 6 5 4 3 2 1

Printed in Dubai

Editorial and design by:
Amber Books Ltd
Bradley's Close
74-77 White Lion Street
London N1 9PF
United Kingdom
www.amberbooks.co.uk

Project Editor: Sarah Uttridge
Design: Brian Rust
Picture Research: Terry Forshaw and Natascha Spargo

ISBN: 978-1-59921-455-9

Library of Congress Cataloging-in-Publication Data is available on file.

Contents

INTRODUCTION

In the words of pirate hunter Sir Henry Keppel (1809–1904):

> As surely as spiders abound where there are nooks and crannies, so have pirates sprung up wherever there is a nest of islands offering creeks and shallows, headlands, rocks and reefs—facilities in short, for lurking, for surprise, for attack, for escape.

Keppel, who went on to become Admiral of the Fleet, hunted pirates in the East, where he helped James Brooke, the "White Rajah" of Sarawak (1803–68), fight piracy in the Malay archipelago. However, his description applied to virtually all pirates wherever and whenever they operated.

Strictly speaking, the word "piracy" denotes boarding and plundering a ship at sea. But most pirates did not stop there. Some vessels carried stupendous wealth, like the Spanish treasure ships that plied the Atlantic Ocean after the middle of the sixteenth century with gold, silver, jewels, and other valuables from mines in their Central and South American colonies. But even these riches were limited compared to the loot to be found in coastal towns and cities or on Caribbean islands like Hispaniola or Cuba. In such places, wealth took other forms, such as the ornaments, chalices, candelabra, and other valuables kept in churches or, sometimes more importantly, the mass of food and other essential supplies in houses or storerooms. Raiding on land as well as by sea was already well established in ancient times when coastal towns

The notorious pirate Edward Teach, alias Blackbeard (left), was finally cornered on Ocracoke Island, North Carolina, by Royal Navy pirate-hunters.

built defensive palisades or fortified walls, hoping to keep the pirates out. They were not always successful, at which point coastal communities simply abandoned their homes and moved inland as far from the marauding pirates as they could get. Living on or near a coast made for a certain vulnerability, which was dramatically exploited in the eighth century CE by the Vikings of Scandinavia. The terrifying Vikings descended on their victims like furies, killing, pillaging, and destroying so thoroughly that their very name inspired panic and terror.

Eventually, the Vikings became settlers in the lands they had once raided. But their sometime contemporaries, the Muslim Barbary pirates of North Africa, also known as the Barbary corsairs, "outlived" the Vikings and remained marauders for another thousand years. Their main hunting ground, the Mediterranean, was the chief focus of piracy until European navigators made their way into the seas and oceans of the world and opened up fresh hunting grounds in America, Africa, and the Indian Ocean.

The Vikings achieved remarkable feats of exploration. Their longboats were re-created in the twentieth century, allowing modern sailors to cross the Atlantic and navigate rivers just as they did centuries earlier.

BUCCANEERS AND PRIVATEERS

Of these venues, the most famous, and the setting for most legends of piracy, lay in Spain's American empire. This stretched from Mexico in the north, across the Caribbean islands, and on to the tip of South America in the south. Here, there were fortunes to be made by raiding such treasure houses as Panama or Maracaibo and Gibraltar in Venezuela, with additional prizes available in the Caribbean islands and the surrounding waters. These were the hunting grounds of Henry Morgan, Blackbeard (Edward Teach), Bartholomew Roberts, and Benjamin Sharpe, some of the most famous pirates of all time, and also of the Brethren of the Coast and others who lived and plundered during the Golden Age of Piracy. These and other Caribbean specialists were known as buccaneers, a name taken from the French word *boucan*, a grill for cooking and curing meat. The Caribbean was also "worked" by semilegal privateers, the ship's captains who carried Letters of Marque and Reprisal from British or French governments. Such papers allowed privateers to capture and plunder vessels on behalf of the governments that employed them. Whatever they were called, these pirates were habitually greedy, predatory, and sadistic. They kidnapped prisoners for ransom. They tortured, they murdered, they destroyed. Yet these same pirates devised a form of liberal-minded contract known nowhere else in the seventeenth and eighteenth centuries; surely the last thing that might be expected of them. By signing the pirate code, also known as Articles of Agreement or Custom of the Coast, pirates pledged themselves to fair shares of the plunder captured, to compensation for injured or crippled companions, and, most surprising of all, to democratic decisions over where next to search for prey and whether to depose an unsatisfactory captain or maroon a troublemaker. Such freedoms seem at odds with their own ferocity and the authoritarian ethos and extreme cruelties that characterized the seventeenth and eighteenth centuries.

The end of piracy, as known and feared until around 1725, came about through the initiatives of the imperial powers: Britain, France, The Netherlands, Spain, and Portugal. They could no longer afford to let pirates make the seas and oceans of the world dangerous. But like similar initiatives across the centuries, success was only temporary. However long it took, piracy always revived. Modern pirates, who reappeared mainly in the East after 1945, are more sophisticated and technologically advanced than ever before, and are now linked to organized crime. The latest pirate chiefs may be less flamboyant than the Henry Morgans or Blackbeards of the past, and much more secretive, but they belong to the same story and, right now, they seem set to take that story far into the future.

Such freedoms seem at odds with their own ferocity and also the authoritarian ethos and extreme cruelties that characterized the seventeenth and eighteenth centuries.

It seems that the punishment of walking the plank, as depicted here, is an invention of Hollywood.

chapter 1

PIRACY IN THE ANCIENT WORLD

Piracy has been a reality of life on Earth ever since humans first constructed ships and journeyed to places, near or far, where booty and treasure were to be found.

In ancient times, the commerce of Egypt, Greece, and Rome was constantly disrupted by pirates who infested the shipping lanes. These pirates lay low, awaiting their prey, among the scattering of islands and the long indentations made by the sea in the coastlines of the eastern Mediterranean. Much of this coast was uninhabited, which was not surprising, when all that was on offer was rocky, barren terrain incapable of supporting large populations. In the winter "off season," pirates might sometimes trade for supplies with the hardier individuals or families who faced the challenges of this demanding environment. But they also needed to spend time and effort scavenging for themselves from what little the local terrain could provide.

More daring pirates, with better seafaring skills —like the Cilicians based in what is now southern Turkey—did brave the storms and heaving seas of the Mediterranean winter to continue plying their

Dionysus, the Greek god of wine, had his own solution to the problem of marauding pirates in the ancient world: as shown here, he turned pirates into peaceable dolphins.

The Ancient Egyptian
Pharaoh Rameses III:
his mortuary temple at
Medinat Habu featured
an inscription describing
an attack in the late
twelfth century BCE by the
pirate Sea Peoples, whom
he later defeated.

trade. But most others ceased activity in the "off season" months, and remained hidden away in creeks and coves or behind long arms of land where it was difficult for their enemies to find them—and dangerous even to try.

The coastline of Lycia, in present-day Anatolia, Turkey, is slashed with narrow inlets and provided with small bays in which the pirates of the day were able to conceal themselves and their ships with ease. At that time, navigators took care to sail within sight of land—a practice known as "coast-hugging"—and this remained a feature of voyaging for almost 3000 years. Coast-hugging, of course, presented a great opportunity to pirates, making it possible for them to surprise a passing vessel and swoop down seemingly out of nowhere to pillage its cargo and seize its crew. That done, the pirates sailed back to the cover of their hiding place where, in or out of "season," they were almost impossible to detect. This was all the more so because a common pirate craft in ancient times was the *myoparo,* a light, swift vessel that was easy to maneuver in shallow coastal waters. Ancient Greek pirates made their winter quarters in the volcanic Aeolian Islands, the modern Lipari Islands, off the north coast of Sicily, which served this purpose for some 2500 years. The Illyrian pirates sheltered in Istria, a peninsula in the Adriatic Sea on the coast of present-day Croatia.

NEW HUNTING SEASON

By the time spring and the new hunting season arrived, the pirate ships were ready to leave their hiding places and return to action. The ships had been careened, refitted, and repaired, their crews were rested and their holds replenished with food and water. Before them lay another season of plundering, kidnapping, enslaving crews or passengers, and generally terrorizing the trade routes and all who sailed them.

This, the standard pattern of Mediterranean piracy, continued for centuries. Pirates and their depredations were a feature of the ancient world long before the advent of classical Greece and Rome. The earliest evidence dates from 1350BCE: an attack made by a pirate ship off the coast of North Africa is recorded on a clay tablet inscribed during the reign of the Egyptian pharaoh Akhenaten (*c.*1362–32BCE). Around 160 years later, in the late twelfth century, another record, this time very detailed and describing a much more serious assault, was included on an inscription at Medinet Habu, the mortuary temple of the pharaoh Rameses III (1184–53BCE) at Thebes in Upper Egypt. The culprits were the mysterious Sea Peoples, a conglomerate of several nationalities, including Philistines, Greeks,

Sardinians, Sicilians, and Lycians. Described in the record as the "Nine Bows," they made their first appearance in Egypt during the reign of the Pharaoh Merenptah (1213–1203BCE). In 1208BCE, they and their Libyan allies mounted a ferocious assault on the Nile Delta. So devastating was it that the area was left "forsaken as pasturage for cattle" and "waste from the time of the ancestors."

Merenptah, however, appears to have been equal to the challenge. An inscription at the Temple of Karnak, near Luxor, records the rousing speech he gave to his court after learning of the invasion.

> I am the ruler who shepherds you...as a father, who preserves his children.... Shall the land be wasted and forsaken at the invasion of every country, while the Nine Bows plunder the borders and rebels invade it every day? They spend their time going about the land, fighting, to fill their bodies daily. They come to the land of Egypt to seek the necessities of their mouths. Their chief is like a dog, a man of boasting without courage...

Part of Rameses III's mortuary temple at Medinat Habu at Thebes in Upper Egypt, a vast complex surrounded by massive mud brick walls. Its eastern gateway was copied from a Syrian fortress.

These were fighting words, and were justified by the battle of Perire in the western Nile Delta, where Merenptah's forces defeated the invaders. As the Karnak inscription relates:

> When (the Egyptian) bowmen went forth, Amun was with them as a shield. After six hours, the...Nine Bows threw down their weapons, abandoned their baggage and dependents and ran for their lives.

Afterward, Merenptah claimed to have killed 6000 soldiers and to have taken 9000 prisoners, a stunning and decisive victory. Or so it would seem. But just over 30 years later, in 1176BCE, during the reign of the pharaoh Rameses III (1184–53BCE) the Sea Peoples were back, this time earning for themselves an even more fearsome reputation for causing chaos. The Ancient Egyptian record presents them not only as pirates raiding in the Nile Delta and along the adjacent coasts, but also as conquerors. It seems that before their return to the Nile Delta, the Sea Peoples destroyed the Hittite empire in eastern Anatolia and sacked several major cities, including Encomi, the capital of Cyprus. The inscription on the outer walls of Medinet Habu, the mortuary temple of Rameses III near Luxor, describes a terrifying foe that launched a sustained and merciless attack, razing vast areas of land.

Aristotle, the great Ancient Greek philosopher, had a slightly cynical view of piracy: He believed that it was just another way of earning a living rather than a crime requiring punishment.

> No land could stand before their arms, from Hatti, Qode, Carchemish, Arzawa, and Alasiya on, being cut off at one time. A camp was set up in one place in Amurru. They desolated its people, and its land was like that which has never come into being. They were coming toward Egypt.... They laid their hands upon the land as far as the circuit of the Earth, their hearts confident and trusting: "Our plans will succeed!"

Against this peril, Rameses prepared his forces:

> I established a boundary in Djahi (near the River Jordan) prepared before them, the local princes, garrison commanders, and Marryanu (warriors). I caused to be prepared the river mouth like a strong wall with warships, galleys and skiffs. They were completely equipped both fore and aft with brave fighters, carrying their weapons and infantry of all the pick of Egypt, being like roaring lions upon the mountains; chariotry with able warriors and all goodly officers whose hands were competent. Their horses quivered in all their limbs, prepared to crush the foreign countries under their hoofs.

When the two sides met, a brutal struggle ensued. Lines of archers

> **A MEMORIAL TO VICTORY**
>
> The victory over the Sea Peoples was the great event of Rameses III's reign, and he made sure that it would be remembered. His mortuary temple at Medinet Habu became virtually a memorial to it, not only in its many inscriptions but also in pictures depicting the vanquished in great detail. One of these features the appearance and weaponry of the Sea Peoples. Some of their warriors carried two spears and a round shield; others preferred a long sword, a spear, and circular shield. Like the Egyptians, the Sea Peoples used chariots pulled by two horses and featuring six-spoke wheels.

unleashed a continuous flow of arrows, preventing the invaders coming ashore. Meanwhile, grappling hooks were flung at the enemy vessels to haul in the enemy's ships. Fierce hand-to-hand fighting followed and the Sea Peoples were resoundingly defeated.

Pictures recording the events included wives and families, shown carrying their possessions with them in ox-carts, an indication that the Sea Peoples were not just pirates and conquerors but also prospective settlers, aiming to displace existing populations and take over their land. The land and sea battles fought by Pharaoh Rameses III and his forces against the Sea Peoples are represented in large, dramatic panoramas. In the sea battle, the Peoples' ships are shown with prows distinctively carved in the shape of birds' heads and with sails, but, curiously, no oars. This has given rise to some speculation that the Sea Peoples had some secret navigation technique unknown to their contemporaries.

A RESPECTABLE PROFESSION

Over seven centuries later, when the Greek historian Thucydides (c.460–c.400BCE) described the pirates of Ancient Greece, it was evident that not much had changed from the days when the Sea Peoples were ravaging the eastern Mediterranean. Although piracy is usually considered a seafaring occupation, the Greek pirates, like the Sea Peoples, were still active on land. They were still stripping towns and villages of everything they could lay their hands on and still terrorizing local populations. What was different, though, was the concept of piracy as a respectable, or at least acceptable, profession. Thucydides wrote:

> This employment did not yet involve any disgrace, but rather brought with it somewhat of glory.

After Thucydides, the Greek philosopher Aristotle (384–322BCE), whose vast literary output included writings on ethics and psychology, regarded piracy as just another means of earning a living. It was, he averred, little different from hunting or fishing.

This intellectual point of view cut no ice with those who suffered most from piracy. The damage wreaked by pirates was a serious, practical matter hampering trade, endangering ships at sea, leaving coastal villages and towns vulnerable, and undermining the ability of rulers to defend themselves, their realms, and

The damage wreaked by pirates was a serious, practical matter hampering trade, endangering ships at sea, and leaving coastal villages and towns vulnerable.

King Minos, the ruler of ancient Crete, was one of the first successful pirate-hunters, establishing a strong naval presence in the eastern Mediterranean to deter the marauders.

their subjects. In a dangerous world, where the rule of law and law courts to back it up had yet to become established as a recognized guarantee of security, a powerful, enterprising ruler was virtually all that stood between society and anarchy. The semi-legendary King Minos of Crete, whose palace at Knossos was built during and after the seventeenth century BCE, set an example long before Rameses III defeated the Sea Peoples.

Minos, according to Thucydides, was the first king to gather his own fleet, gain control of eastern Mediterranean waters, and rule the Cyclades islands in the Aegean Sea. From this position of strength, Minos cleared out the pirates and restored the flow of revenue to his kingdom, which piracy had previously blocked. Thucydides also suggests that the Carians, who originated in mainland Greece and provided the manpower for the Minoan fleet, doubled as pirates. Minos, it seems, tolerated this sideline for a while, but when it got out of hand, he expelled the Carians from Crete.

EXCAVATIONS SUPPORT HISTORICAL RECORDS

After 1900, when the English archaeologist Sir Arthur Evans began excavating the Palace of Knossos and its surrounding area, his findings revealed—by inference—proof of Thucydides' account. Minoan Crete was an ancient civilization marked by fabulous wealth and a standard of living far in advance of its time. Yet, as Evans discovered, these riches were relatively untouched even in Cretan towns with no protective walls. This would have been impossible unless pirates and other marauders were kept away by a strong naval presence. Similarly, the trade between Crete and Ancient Egypt could not have continued as it did unless Cretan ships retained control of the trans-Mediterranean sea lanes.

On Crete, the risk of pirate attack, though very much reduced, was not entirely eliminated. At Knossos in late Minoan times, the northern approaches to the royal palace had to be fortified in case of invasion by one of the numerous pirate bands operating out of southern Asia Minor. But sadly, around 1400BCE, the tsunami caused by a massive eruption of Thera, on Santorini, a group of volcanic islands 62 miles (100km) from Crete, destroyed the Minoan civilization and, with it, the anti-pirate controls once exerted by King Minos.

The Cretan king's place as guardian of the eastern Mediterranean was not filled—at least not effectively—for a very long time. Once Cretan control had gone, the area became a dangerous place, ravaged by invaders, raiders, and freebooters from Samos (a hotbed of piracy in the Aegean Sea), from Asia Minor and from elsewhere along the Mediterranean coasts. Before long, passengers embarking on voyages in the Aegean did so knowing that they were risking their freedom, their possessions, and sometimes their lives. Pirates from Tyre, Phoenicia and elsewhere did not scruple to board ships, seize the women and boys, and carry them off to sell in the slave markets. Some pirates moored at ports where, ostensibly, they were welcome, and then proceeded to snatch their victims off the streets.

In the open sea or close to a deserted coast, there was nothing to prevent a marauding pirate ship from boarding and capturing a smaller vessel. The identity of the pirates varied, but the outcome was always destructive. Turks usually chose to pillage a captured ship. Pirates from North Africa took the youngest men

The temple at Knossos, the chief city of Minoan Crete. The excavations carried out by Sir Arthur Evans between 1899 and 1935 revealed an amazingly advanced standard of living, which included the provision of running water.

aboard as slaves. The Greeks concentrated on seizing cargo and, it seems, did not care if they were robbing their own people. Meanwhile, on the shore, the coast of Attica in central Greece became a regular target for pirates who were possibly the descendants of King Minos' Carians.

Some moves were made to protect ships and coasts, and the navies of Athens and other Greek city-states played their part in making the Mediterranean a safer place. Coastal defense systems were put in place, and towns and villages were either fortified or built further inland, away from coasts. Some were sited on hilltops in an attempt to keep them out of the reach of pirates.

Another factor also helped to counter piracy. Acceptance, even admiration, of pirates no longer existed. The Delphic oracle, founded in the eighth century BCE, declared against piracy and demanded that the Greeks adopt a higher morality. Although the oracle's pronouncements set a more upright tone for many Greeks, these were a tall order when it came to pirates and their motivations. Commercial rivalries and jealousies, personal feuds and vendettas got in the way of peaceful or honorable dealings and the standard of Greek morality declined sharply once booty, gain, and the chance to triumph over hated rivals were in the mix.

The disappearance of the most fearsome Mediterranean pirates had little effect on the basic problem, as many others remained at large and some local rulers found a convenient use for them.

The Greeks, one of the most fearless and adventurous people in the ancient world, sought to explore and settle territories in the western Mediterranean and possibly beyond. But even they were prevented from planting their presence too far west from home in case they fell foul of the Tyrrhenians. The Greeks were not alone. Fear of the Tyrrhenians seemed to be universal. For instance, on Delos, the smallest of the Cyclades, the inhabitants took out a large loan in 298BCE to build defenses and fortify their island as safeguards against these pirates.

The Tyrrhenians did not have it all their own way. In the fourth century BCE, one of them, a pirate named Postumius, was captured by Timoleon of Corinth (*c*.411–337BCE) together with 12 galleys he had used to create havoc in the seas around Sicily. Sicily was in the purview of Rome and though not yet the great imperial power it later became, Rome already possessed great influence in Italy and its adjacent islands. By this time, Rome had already taken steps to prevent Italian pirates making a nuisance of themselves in Italian territorial waters. In Volume Eight of his *History of Rome*, the historian Livy (59–17BCE) recounts how the Romans banned the warlike Volscians of Antium (Anzio) from putting out to

NOTORIOUS PIRATES

Probably the most notorious pirates in the ancient Mediterranean were the Tyrrehenians, who first appeared in the record in the early fourth century BCE. They were based on Lemnos, one of the Aegean islands, but also operated around the Italian coasts. Tyrrehenian attacks were so destructive and their greed for plunder so intense that their name became a synonym for "pirate." Evidence of Tyrrehenian activities may be fragmentary, but there is no doubt of their ferocity. In 325–24BCE, the Athenians were so concerned about the danger Tyrrehenians posed to their grain supplies that they stationed a squadron of naval vessels at the port of Adria, in southern central Italy, to guard traders and their corn ships. The arrangement was meant to be permanent.

sea, thus preventing a great deal of raiding, robbing, and destruction. Precisely how or, indeed, if the Romans slipped up in the case of the pirate Postumius is not known, but one Greek ruler, Demeter I of Macedon (337–283BCE), sent a sharply worded missive to Rome criticizing its rulers for their lack of control over their own people and calling on the Roman authorities to impose a greater degree of restraint upon them.

Fortunately, it seems that the Tyrrhenians were not long on the pirate scene. In the early third century BCE, according to an inscription on the island of Rhodes, there was some sort of confrontation off the coast of Sicily or southern Italy between the pirates and the Rhodians. After that, it seems that the Tyrrhenians vanished from the record.

But the disappearance of the most fearsome of Mediterranean pirates had little effect on the basic problem, as many others remained at large, and some local rulers found a convenient use for them. At a time when armies were largely made up of mercenaries, it was all one to the pirates whether they marauded on their own behalf or joined the forces of some ruler needing reinforcements to wage war. For example, around 8000 pirates enlisted in the army of Demetrius I of Macedon for an assault on Rhodes, which took place in 305–04BCE. To a considerable extent, Demetrius depended on pirates to maintain his naval supremacy in the eastern Mediterranean, but inevitably, they proved a tough lot to handle. By nature, they were plunderers and killers, and Demetrius used them as such in his attack on Rhodes, where the pirate vessels were used to ravage the island's coasts. Demetrius also hired large numbers of pirates for his garrison at the port of Ephesus (present-day Izmir, in Turkey) and employed more than one "arch-pirate" who combined service to the Macedonian leader with looting, pillaging, and massacring on his own account.

Titus Livius, known as Livy to English-speakers, was an influential Roman historian. He wrote a 142-book history of Rome and served at the court of the first Roman Emperor, Augustus.

INSECURITY IN TOWNS

Unsurprisingly, with rogues like this on the loose and few, if any, permanent defenses against them, there was a chronic sense of insecurity in the towns and villages close to the Mediterranean coasts. Several emergency calls for help were made by beleaguered communities. One of them, Thera in the Cyclades, was in

The island of Crete in the eastern Mediterranean had been a center for successful pirate-hunting until its Minoan civilization was destroyed by a tsunami in around 1400BCE. Afterward, Crete acquired its own pirates.

grave danger of attack by Allarian or Cretan pirates and appealed to the Egyptians for rescue. Under cover of darkness, the Egyptians sent a well-armed force of soldiers, who landed on Thera out of sight of the pirates and then joined the islanders in driving the miscreants back to their ships. Not long afterward, between 228BCE and 225BCE, the Egyptians sent a detachment of infantry, cavalry, and siege machines, complete with specialized crews, to the island of Samothrace in the northeast of the Aegean Sea, where priceless temple treasures needed a strong guard to cope with pirates who were aiming to seize them.

Unfortunately, emergency services that could intervene at trouble spots like Thera and Samothrace were only one-off cures. What was needed, as King Minos of Crete had shown fourteen centuries earlier, was a strong naval force that could police the waters and coasts of the Mediterranean Sea. The island of Rhodes, which was itself susceptible to pirate attack, took the lead here and, after around 200BCE, emerged as an important naval power with a cohesive policing policy that could ensure the safety of navigators.

RHODES FIGHTS BACK

Ever since the city of Rhodes was founded in around 408BCE, Rhodian traders had carried their cargoes in armed merchantmen, which were able to beat off most onslaughts from pirate vessels. Rhodian guardships made long and regular cruises among the Aegean islands. Rhodian patrols provided effective protection for the ships and commerce of the islands and once chased off an Illyrian fleet heading for targets in the Aegean. It seems that the Illyrians, themselves no mean exponents in the business of piracy, learned their lesson, for there is no other mention of their fleet in the record.

The Rhodians furthered their campaign by making treaties with other states to ensure mutual assistance in suppressing piracy. One of these treaties was made in around 200–197BCE, between Rhodes and Hierapytna, a respectable town on Crete, where, otherwise, piracy was practically endemic. The treaty stipulated that Hierapytna must give its support to Rhodes on both land and sea. Should any pirates be captured, they and their ships were to be handed over to the Rhodians. Any spoils taken were to be divided equally between Rhodes, Hierapytna, and any allies they might have at the time. If Hierapytna suffered assault by allies of the pirates, the Rhodians were bound by duty to assist the Cretan city.

Unfortunately, the Rhodian fleet was never ubiquitous enough to give blanket coverage to the Aegean area and its hundreds of islands, and when the Rhodians' backs were turned, the pirates made the most of it. On one occasion, pirates came by night to the Aegean town of Aegiale on the island of Amorgos and seized

Between 264BCE and 146BCE, Rome fought three wars against its great rival Carthage. Rome eventually triumphed and without Carthage in the way, was able to put paid to piracy in the Mediterranean.

more than 30 men, women, and slaves. The pirates commandeered a boat moored in the harbor to take the prisoners away, but the pirate leader, Socleidas, was persuaded to hold 28 of the captives to ransom while the remaining two stayed on board as hostages. According to an inscription on Naxos, a greater number of captives, 280, was held to ransom by Aetolian pirates from central Greece. The Aetolians operated a type of "protection racket" to induce Aegean cities to join their Aetolian League, first formed in 370BCE: By joining, the cities gained immunity from Aetolian raids and reprisals. By this means, the Aetolians came to dominate all of central Greece apart from Attica by the end of the third century BCE.

The Aetolian pirates were vilified for their cruelty, greed, and dishonesty, but they were little worse than Cretan pirates who excelled at kidnapping women and conducting guerrilla warfare. According to the historian Polybius (205–123BCE), they were experts at staging ambushes, night assaults, and surprise attacks.

Queen Teuta of Illyria was a thorn in the side of the Romans for a long time. Here, the Queen is shown in 213BCE ordering Roman ambassadors to be killed.

GEOGRAPHY CREATES PIRATES

The geography of Crete itself also played a part in suiting its people to a life of warfare and piracy. Crete was in many ways a miniature version of Greece, offering a similarly taxing environment of mountains and valleys where life was

hard and much effort was needed to wrest a living from the unforgiving terrain. Territory like this produced tough, hardy warriors capable of great ferocity and endurance. As a people, they were resistant to hardship and well suited to the life of mercenaries—or pirates.

The heavily indented northern coastline of Crete afforded numerous hiding places for pirate vessels. Crete was also the sort of place where young men left home as soon as they could and sought more lucrative and exciting employment overseas. This helped account for the large numbers of Cretans who became mercenaries and soldiers serving in the armies of Egypt, the city-states of Greece and any other rulers who cared to employ them. In the eastern Mediterranean, Cretan mercenaries served in all the wars of the third and second centuries BCE, and while they were at it, they served themselves as pirates at every opportunity.

Crete, therefore, assumed great importance in the foreign policy of the rulers of other Aegean islands. Some even made it a priority to acquire a foothold on Crete. In 217BCE, it was the turn of Philip V of Macedon (238–179BCE) to exert his influence over Crete. Philip set about making life difficult for Rhodes by stirring up serious outbreaks of piracy on Crete, causing more trouble for the Rhodian pirate-hunters than their limited resources could handle. In 204BCE, at Philip's behest, a Rhodian fleet was destroyed by his Greek ally, Hieracleides, who also contrived to set fire to the arsenal on Rhodes, for good measure.

Before long, thanks to Philip, the entire Aegean was in a state of emergency, so much so that it fully occupied the Rhodian pirate-hunters for a full two years. Meanwhile, Philip was able to proceed with his expansionist plans, which included replacing Roman influence along the eastern shore of the Adriatic and the coastline of North Africa. The Romans had been active in the Mediterranean since 264BCE, when their First Punic War with Carthage, which lay across the water on the Tunisian coast, drew them into the politics of the region. The three Punic Wars, which ended in 201BCE with the decisive defeat of Carthage, represented Rome's first foray into empire and brought them into direct conflict with Philip V.

PHILIP'S FORCES THRASHED BY ROME

The Romans were already the conquerors of all Italy, with an army that was already the best in the world at that time and would soon be the most successful. They viewed Philip as an upstart and dealt very smartly with him. In 200BCE, immediately after the fall of Carthage, they declared war and within three years Philip and his forces were beaten. In the peace treaty that followed, Philip was confined to Macedonia and was obliged to surrender his fleet. This put an end to his overseas ambitions, and with Rome victorious, Rhodes was again able to retrieve something of its former supremacy in the Greek islands. In practical terms, of course, Rhodes was now under the tutelage of Rome. But with their experience, local alliances, and trade links in the eastern Mediterranean, the Rhodians were well suited to freeing the Romans for an important task in the west—the protection of Spain, a colony of Carthage taken over by Rome.

Even for the mighty Romans, this was a formidable task. Around the year 181BCE, the sea routes to Spain were being severely threatened by the Iguani pirates, one of the Ligurian tribes who originated in northwest Italy and southeast France. At this point in time, the Iguani were based close to Genoa.

Territory like this produced tough, hardy warriors capable of great ferocity and endurance. As a people, they were resistant to hardship and well suited to the life of mercenaries— or pirates.

Wild and intensely aggressive, they were once classed as "barbarians" by Hesiod, a Greek poet of the eighth century BCE. Raiding and pillaging—and pirating—were an integral part of their lifestyle. Their manners had hardly improved centuries later—they were familiar foes of long standing before they began to interfere with Roman interests in the western Mediterranean. In fact, the Iguani had given Rome so much trouble that the historian Livy (59BCE–17CE) called their territory a regular training ground for the Roman Army.

The reach of the Iguani was so extensive that their pirates endangered trading ships along the eastern coast of Spain as far as Gibraltar at the western entrance to the Mediterranean. But this time, when the Romans acted, the upshot was not just another frontier war. With vital land and sea routes to Spain at stake, it was a must-win situation for Rome. This was why one of Rome's best generals, the tough, experienced consul Lucius Aemilius Paullus (c229–160BCE), was given command of the Roman Army, which mounted a vigorous onslaught against the Iguani. Superior Roman arms, discipline, strategy, and tactics prevailed and the Iguani were crushed. Subsequently, they were forced to surrender 32 of their pirate vessels.

The Romans overran several Illyrian coastal towns and advanced inland, where they used a strong show of force to impress on the inhabitants precisely who was boss.

SAFEGUARDING SPAIN

This, though, was not the end of the matter. Other Ligurian tribes continued to resist, and the Romans were still embroiled with them some 60 years later, in 123BCE, when the sea routes to Spain were once more in peril. This time, the danger came from pirates preying on the Balearic islands, the archipelago off the east coast of Spain. The island inhabitants had the reputation of being peaceful, but they did not shrink from collaborating with the local pirates and taking advantage of the booty and other gains that piracy afforded. The Romans replied by occupying the four Balearic main islands and founding two towns, Pollentia and Palma de Majorca. In addition, some three thousand settlers were shipped in from Spain to secure the islands for Rome.

Safeguarding Spain also provided protection for the west coast of Italy. However, the Italian east coast was likewise endangered by pirates—in this case, the tribes inhabiting the shores of Illyria (the Balkan peninsula) across the Adriatic Sea. These shores were thoroughgoing badlands, peopled by the

THE QUEEN TURNS A BLIND EYE TO PIRACY
The Illyrians and their formidable queen, Teuta, were an especially taxing problem. Teuta's invariable answer to complaints about the behavior of Illyrian pirates was that rulers in Illyria did not normally interfere with the sea-going activities of their subjects.

As their queen knew perfectly well, Illyrian pirates were savage plunderers and raiders. They killed and captured large numbers of Italian traders and were adept at cunning tricks. On one occasion, they anchored near the town of Messania in the Peloponnese and persuaded the townspeople to trade with them. While the trade was going on, the Illyrians suddenly seized several Messanians, rushed them on board their ship and sailed away, bound, no doubt, for the slave markets.

predatory Istrians, Dalmatians, Ligurians, as well as Illyrians and others, all of whom were barely civilized, at least by Roman standards of the day.

ROMAN PROTESTS

For a while, the Romans showed unusual forbearance: instead of retaliating against the Illyrians, they tried diplomacy and polite protests. Eventually, though, Roman patience gave out. A fully equipped fleet of 200 ships, 20,000 infantry, and 200 cavalry was dispatched to teach the Illyrians, and their queen, a lesson. Pirates and other miscreants were threatened with savage punishments, such as decapitation, crucifixion, and being torn apart by wild beasts, upon capture.

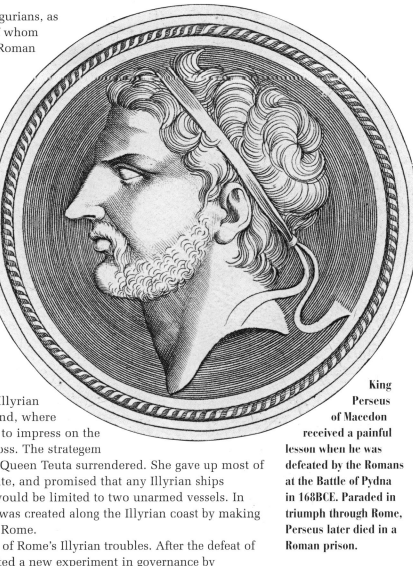

King Perseus of Macedon received a painful lesson when he was defeated by the Romans at the Battle of Pydna in 168BCE. Paraded in triumph through Rome, Perseus later died in a Roman prison.

The Romans overran several Illyrian coastal towns and advanced inland, where they used a strong show of force to impress on the inhabitants precisely who was boss. The strategem worked. In the spring of 228BCE, Queen Teuta surrendered. She gave up most of her realm, paid appropriate tribute, and promised that any Illyrian ships putting out to sea in the future would be limited to two unarmed vessels. In addition, a controlling presence was created along the Illyrian coast by making several towns directly subject to Rome.

This, though, was not the end of Rome's Illyrian troubles. After the defeat of Queen Teuta, the Romans attempted a new experiment in governance by appointing an amenable client ruler to control a newly conquered, if dangerous, province. Unfortunately, the man chosen by the Romans—Demetrius of Pharos—proved to be a disaster. Scerdilaidas, the Greek "minder" picked by the Romans to keep an eye on the untrustworthy Demetrius, was not much better. Scerdilaidas was himself a pirate and it was not long before he had allied himself with Demetrius to carry out a plundering raid on Cape Malea in the Peloponnese. With Demetrius and Scerdilaidas in control, Illyria turned virtually overnight into hostile territory. The Romans soon took control from them, with the army they sent to the "enemy" coast in 219BCE.

The Roman forces smashed their way into Dimale, a supposedly impregnable coastal fortress, and scattered Demetrius' terrified supporters. Next, the Romans headed for Demetrius' home base of Pharos, where they soon destroyed the defending forces and the city along with them. The game was up for Demetrius,

25

who fled to Macedonia and the protection of Philip V. That done, Rome established a protectorate over southern Illyria and the northern part of the adjacent state, Epiros. Between them, Illyria and Epiros in their new Roman guise were there to keep watch on Macedon and its king.

Scerdilaidas, meanwhile, had returned to his former occupation and staged several pirate raids around Cape Malea. He offered his services and his fleet to the Aetolians and to Philip V. However, he quarreled with both of them and afterward, surprisingly, became an ally of Rome. Even though Scerdilaidas was at heart a cynical opportunist who had only a slight acquaintance with the virtues of loyalty and commitment, his alliance with Rome proved remarkably successful. Appointed the new client king of Illyria, Scerdilaidas stood by Rome when King Philip was planning an invasion of Italy and brought up his son, Pleuratus, to follow the same policy.

It seems that Scerdilaidas became a new man. As an ally of Rome, he refrained from staging pirate raids. Nor were there any during the reign of his son, who came to the throne as King Pleuratus II in 205BCE. Like his father,

A panoramic view of the Taurus Mountains in Turkey. This was the home of the Cilicians, who were the last pirates to challenge the mighty Romans. They were thrashed by Rome in 66BCE.

THE VENGEANCE OF ROME

Roman vengeance was swift and total. The praetor Anicius led a large army into Illyria to join up with Roman forces already stationed there. With the tacit consent of Genthius' subjects, who were thoroughly disillusioned with him, the Romans crushed the king's forces. Their resistance lasted only 30 days before Genthius had to surrender. Afterward, Genthius was taken to Rome with his wife and children, and it seems that he suffered the ultimate humiliation. He was paraded through the streets to the jeers of the watching crowds. Subsequently, Genthius was banished, his former kingdom was dismembered, and ultimately, Illyria became a province of the Roman Empire.

he remained faithful to Rome, but the crucial weakness in this arrangement became apparent after he died in around 180BCE. Pleuratus was succeeded by his cruel and despotic son, Genthius, who was too fond of wine for his own, or his kingdom's, good. Unwisely, the Romans had taken their eye off Illyria while the trusted Pleuratus was in charge. As a result, they neglected Illyria's trouble-spot potential and almost as soon as Genthius succeeded to the throne he faced a crisis. There was a widespread uprising in Dalmatia, in the northern part of his kingdom, and Genthius was too weak and indecisive to do anything about it.

ROME STEPS IN

Unable to trust Genthius, the Romans sent a fleet of ships, complete with troops, to keep him under surveillance. By this time, the Illyrian coast was in a ferment as pirates made repeated forays, and the territory of Issa, one of several cities originally founded by the Greeks, was pillaged and plundered. For a time, Genthius was able to keep the Romans quiet by bribing the agent they sent to his court to return to Rome with a favorable report. The Illyrian king procrastinated for several more years, until finally in 168BCE, he declared against Rome, allied himself to Macedon, and imprisoned the Roman ambassadors to his court.

Genthius' ally, King Perseus of Macedon, who succeeded to the throne on the death of Philip V, his father, in 179BCE, received the same treatment 11 years later. Led by Lucius Aemilius Paullus, victor over the Ligurian Iguani pirates 13 years earlier, the Romans met the Macedonian forces at the Aegean port of Pydna, which lay on the River Aeson, north of the sacred Mount Olympus. The night before, on June 21 168BCE, there was an eclipse of the Moon, which both sides, equally superstitious, interpreted as a portent. The Romans considered it favorable. The Macedonians, thrown into consternation, predicted defeat. And so it proved. On the afternoon of June 22, the Macedonian phalanx remained unbroken as it advanced over the flat terrain near the river. But when the terrain became uneven, it lost alignment and the Romans, taking advantage of the gaps that appeared, penetrated the phalanx and broke it up.

Some 20,000 Macedonians were killed, and 11,000 captured. The Romans themselves lost 1000 men. King Perseus managed to escape with a few other survivors, but he later surrendered and, like Genthius, was paraded through the streets of Rome in triumph. Perseus died a prisoner four years later at

> On the afternoon of June 22, there was an eclipse of the Moon, which both sides, equally superstitious, interpreted as a portent.

Alba Fucens, a fortified town near Rome. Macedon was broken up and became the Roman imperial province of Macedonia in 146BCE. This was the end of Greek independence because, after 146BCE, one Greek city-state after another submitted to Rome. The Greeks would not know independence again for another 2000 years.

PIRACY REIGNS UNCHALLENGED IN THE AEGEAN

But even the collapse of Greece was not to signal the end of piracy in the ancient Mediterranean. Over the centuries, the demise of the Carthaginian empire and the Seleucid empire in Mesopotamia, together with the decline of Ancient Egypt, had done away with powers strong enough to challenge piracy in the Aegean. Instead, the pirates were able to claim greater and greater freedom to ravage the coastlines, islands, and shipping and to spread trepidation and terror among vulnerable communities. By this time, though, experience had taught the Romans that prevention, in the form of client kings or guardian fleets, was not better than cure. Only blanket methods would do to expunge the scourge of piracy and lawlessness. When the Romans embarked on their next anti-pirate campaign, total control or total destruction were their ultimate weapons.

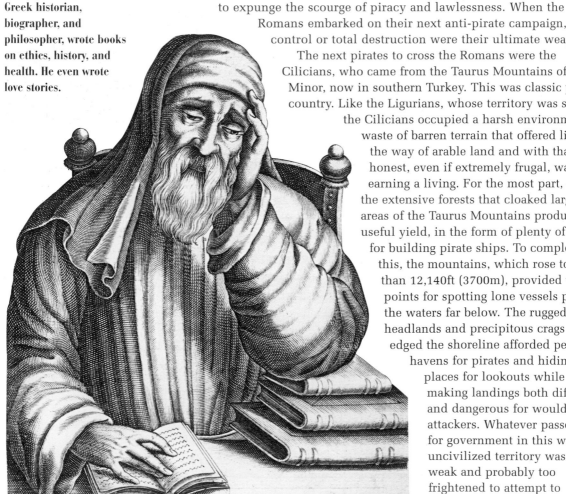

Plutarch, the renowned Greek historian, biographer, and philosopher, wrote books on ethics, history, and health. He even wrote love stories.

The next pirates to cross the Romans were the Cilicians, who came from the Taurus Mountains of Asia Minor, now in southern Turkey. This was classic pirate country. Like the Ligurians, whose territory was similar, the Cilicians occupied a harsh environment, a waste of barren terrain that offered little in the way of arable land and with that, honest, even if extremely frugal, ways of earning a living. For the most part, only the extensive forests that cloaked large areas of the Taurus Mountains produced a useful yield, in the form of plenty of wood for building pirate ships. To complement this, the mountains, which rose to more than 12,140ft (3700m), provided vantage points for spotting lone vessels plying the waters far below. The rugged headlands and precipitous crags that edged the shoreline afforded perfect havens for pirates and hiding places for lookouts while making landings both difficult and dangerous for would-be attackers. Whatever passed for government in this wild, uncivilized territory was too weak and probably too frightened to attempt to suppress the pirates. In this

context, piracy enjoyed a bonanza and pirate navies became the principal sea power in the eastern Mediterranean. Yet the Romans hesitated for a long time before taking action. The delay may have been due to a singular benefit afforded by piracy. The chief "goods" in which the pirates dealt were slaves, and a regular supply of slaves was needed not only in Rome but in other Mediterranean cities that had achieved a degree of affluence. Rome was the pirates' principal market, because Roman landowners ran large plantations, particularly in Sicily, where hundreds of slaves were required. The statistics were startling. The island of Delos in the Cyclades became the hub of the slave trade, with other thriving markets at Alexandria in Egypt and Rhodes. It was said that up to 10,000 slaves could be bought and sold at these markets in a single day. To maintain the delivery of slaves, some cities, such as Phaselis, on the coast of Lycia, made deals with the pirates and another town, Side, now in Turkey, put its dockyards at their disposal.

A reconstruction of Delos, one of the Cyclades islands and sited in the center of the group, was first inhabited as long ago as 3000BCE. Delos was an important center for the slave trade.

THE SLAVE TRADE

The vastly lucrative slave trade, and the freedom with which they conducted it, emboldened the pirates and fed their greed. This led them to extend their activities westward across the Mediterranean, from Cyprus and eastern Turkey, to Africa and as far as Roman-ruled Spain. The more extensive their raids, the bolder the Cilicians became. Then in 75BCE, they overreached themselves near the Aegean island of Pharmakussa, capturing a ship sailing to Rhodes and taking its passengers and crew prisoner. One of the prisoners was Gaius Julius Caesar, then a 25-year-old aristocrat from a distinguished Roman family who was traveling to Rhodes to study rhetoric. The Cilicians obviously failed to recognize the prestige of the prize that had fallen into their hands. They demanded a ransom of 20 talents, the rough equivalent of £1200. Caesar was highly insulted. Believing that he was worth more than that, he demanded that the pirates ask for 50 talents, or £3000. What was more, he insisted, he would pay that amount straight away.

Caesar sent his servants ashore to raise the ransom from local villages, and while he awaited their return, he promised the Cilicians that, after he was free, he would hunt them down and see that they were executed. The Cilicians, it seems, considered Caesar to be an arrogant little upstart who was joking with them, but the young Roman was as good as his word. After a confinement lasting 40 days, the ransom was paid and he was free. At Miletos, a seaport now in Turkey, Caesar gathered together a modest fleet and returned to Pharmakussa, to find that the Cilicians were still there.

The Cilicians were soon captured and Caesar took them to Pergamum (Turkey), where they were imprisoned. Caesar went to the Roman governor and demanded that they be executed forthwith. Either the governor refused, preferring to sell the Cilicians as slaves, or he was not sufficiently quick on the draw for Caesar. The upshot was that Caesar personally ordered the Cilicians to be crucified. It seems, too, that he also took back the ransom he had paid.

This, though, was a small success compared to the continuing depredations of the Cilician pirates. Their confidence was such that they built watchtowers and beacons on the coasts to guard their arsenals and their harbors. Then, they made a big mistake. They began attacking towns on the Italian coast and even plundered Ostia, the port of Rome. When the pirate peril came that close to home, the Romans could no longer close their eyes to it. In 75BCE, the consul Servilius Isauricus (died 44BCE) commanded a Roman army that attacked the pirates' naval bases in Cilicia. Unfortunately, Servilius failed to finish the job, and eight years later an emergency arose when Rome's corn supply ran short after the pirates interfered with the shipping routes from Egypt, its main supplier.

> **One of the prisoners was Gaius Julius Caesar, then a 25-year-old aristocrat from a distinguished Roman family.**

POMPEY TAKES ON THE PIRACY PROBLEM

But at long last, the Romans woke up to the fact that they had been merely tickling at the problem. As a result, in 67BCE, they came out in tremendous force, massively armed and led by their greatest general of the time, Gnaeus Pompeius, better known as Pompey. The force voted to Pompey by the Senate was so enormous that aristocratic senators feared giving one man such overwhelming power and attempted, unsuccessfully, to prevent it. Pompey was to receive absolute control over the Mediterranean and its coasts, extending more than 50 miles (80 km) inland, thus making his powers superior to every other military leader in the area. His forces comprised a fleet of 500 battleships, 120,000 infantry, and some 5000 cavalry.

Pompey spent the winter of 67–66BCE planning his campaign. He divided the Mediterranean into 13 separate regions, and put each of them under the command of a legate, who carried the rank of general. Pompey's campaign got under way in the spring of 66BCE and within only 40 days, the pirates were cleared out of the western Mediterranean. Turning east, Pompey headed for the coast of Cilicia, where he sought out the pirates' strongholds and harbors, and destroyed their fleets. The suddenness and speed of the campaign seemed to stun the surviving pirates into submission. When Pompey announced an amnesty, many gave themselves up. Many others became prisoners. The campaign was all over within a mere three months.

The Cilicians might now have expected savage punishments, but instead there was no revenge and no extermination. The Romans had long since discovered that offering defeated enemies the Roman way of life in Roman-style cities, setting aside land for them to cultivate as their own, and even giving them citizenship, were effective ways of winning their allegiance and ensuring their loyalty. These were offers that the Cilician and other pirates, like many peoples vanquished by the Romans both before and after them, could not refuse.

Nevertheless, what ultimately tamed them was Rome in its mightiest guise. Flexing her superpower muscles, Rome brought down a force that had once enjoyed centuries of supremacy, holding entire populations in thrall, thumbing its nose at empires, stealing several fortunes in plunder, and terrorizing the Mediterranean for more than 40 generations.

Pompey also known as Gnaeus Pompeius, was the great hero of the hour in Rome after he ended piracy in the Mediterranean in 66BCE. Here he is, four years later, being elected consul of Rome.

chapter 2

VIKING AND BARBARY PIRATES

On January 8, 793CE, the slim outline of a ship carrying a large, square sail appeared on the horizon, heading for the island of Lindisfarne off the northeast coast of England. As it drew closer, the round shields lining the ship's side became visible. So did its fierce-looking dragon- or serpent-headed prow. The oarsmen, about 60 in number, were all pulling strongly for the shore, their helmets glinting in the winter sunshine. Lindisfarne, also known as Holy Island, lay some 1–2 miles (3km) out in the North Sea and was a center of Christian learning, known and revered throughout Europe. It was also a repository for the stupendous wealth amassed by the Church over the years, and the monks who lived in the island's abbey were there to guard it.

Ships had visited Lindisfarne from time to time, bringing food, wine, and other supplies or new recruits for the abbey. But this ship must have seemed different. Hugging the coast for safety had been the rule for voyaging ever since ships first put out to sea, but the vessel now approaching the shore so rapidly was not following that rule. Instead, it

For the Vikings, crossing the North Sea out of sight of land was an achievement, but a dangerous one. For this reason, they lashed three ships together during the voyage.

appeared to be coming directly from the open sea, which meant that for most of its voyage to England, it must have sailed out of sight of land. In the eighth century CE, this feat was unheard of and it added to the horror that followed when the ship swept up the beach and its crew leapt ashore. Yelling terrifying war cries and brandishing murderous-looking spears, axes, and swords, they made a rush for the church, cutting down any monk who tried to stop them. Once inside, they set about stripping out all the treasures they could lay their hands on. They tore gold, silver, and jeweled ornaments off the walls and grabbed cups, plates, crucifixes, and other sacred emblems off the altars. They ransacked chests and cupboards and scattered the contents over the floor. When, at last, they were done, the raiders drowned or slaughtered most of the monks who had survived the initial assault and carried off others, mostly the younger, fitter men, for sale in the European slave markets.

The raid on the island of Lindisfarne or Holy Island in 793CE was the first appearance of the Vikings off the coast of Britain. It was, however, by no means the last.

ENTER THE VIKINGS

This was how the Vikings of Scandinavia made their first, terrifying, appearance in *The Anglo Saxon Chronicle*, the mammoth history of early medieval England. Written by generations of clerics, the *Chronicle* included strongly superstitious influences and was pervaded by a sense of the sins of humanity that had brought the Viking catastrophe upon them. The entry for the year 793CE ran thus:

In this year, fierce, foreboding omens came over the land of Northumbria.... There were excessive whirlwinds, lightning storms and fiery dragons were seen flying in the sky. These signs were followed by great famine, and shortly after in the same year, on January 8, the ravaging of heathen men destroyed God's church at Lindisfarne through brutal robbery and slaughter.

Like all churchmen, whoever wrote that was well aware of a fearful forecast in the Biblical Book of Jeremiah, who prophesied:

Out of the North an evil shall break forth over all the inhabitants of the land.

Another, equally apocalyptic observation, came from the Northumbrian scholar Alcuin (*c*.737–804CE), who wrote,

Never before has such a horror appeared in Britain such as we have suffered from the heathen...there is the beginning of woe and calamity.

The "beginning of woe and calamity" had in reality, commenced a few years earlier, in 787CE, when three Viking vessels arrived off the Dorset coast from Denmark to see what England had to offer. Tempting tales of English wealth had already spread around Europe and the Danish visitors soon realized how accurate they were. England was a treasurehouse of fertile fields and valuable minerals. The stunning wealth of English churches and monasteries was there for all to see. Scandinavia was no match for all this affluence. Wresting a living from its hard, unyielding soil was a gruelling task. There was too little land to go round, and Scandinavia was overpopulated. The Viking custom of primogeniture, in which the first-born in a family inherited all its wealth and property, left too many younger brothers without prospects. In this context, the Danish visitors had no problem making up their minds. For good measure, they sent in a landing party that killed the reeve who confronted them, then plundered the neighborhood and sailed away. The entry in *The Anglo Saxon Chronicle* expressed no doubt about the Danes' ultimate ambitions. The entry for 787CE read:

> These were the first ships of the Danish men that sought the land of the English nation.

They were, of course, not the last. The raid on Lindisfarne that followed four years later was only a prelude to a whole succession of Viking brutalities. Only a year later, the Vikings attacked the monastery at Jarrow further down the northeast coast from Lindisfarne. But they did not have things all their own way. As *The Anglo Saxon Chronicle* records:

> The heathens in Northumbria ravaged and robbed (the) monastery at Jarrow. There, some of their war leaders were killed and also some of their ships were broken up in bad weather and many drowned. Some came alive to shore and were quickly killed...

This setback did not deter the Vikings from further onslaughts. Indeed, Norwegian Vikings launched the first of many attacks on Ireland, ravaging the island of Lambay, in Dublin Bay. After one of their battles, the Vikings revealed a disgusting habit that shocked the Irish, who were themselves no mean marauders. They cooked a victory meal in a caldron placed on top of the bodies of their vanquished enemies. Either that, or they stuck spits into the corpses and roasted their food on them.

The same year saw Viking raiders swarm onto the island of Iona, where they pillaged and plundered its treasures with murderous efficiency. In 798CE, it was the turn of the Isle of Man; and in 802CE and 806CE, the Vikings returned to Iona.

The Vikings gave their warships a terrifying appearance, with shields ranged along the sides and a ferocious animal head at the prow. A warship also had a slim outline, unlike the wider Viking trading ships.

35

WE WILL PAY YOU TO STAY AWAY
When raiding, the Vikings killed cattle, trussed them up, and took them off as food, together with the other booty they loaded into their vessels. Occasionally, if they knew of more prizes inland, the Vikings stole horses and rode out into the countryside to ravage more towns and villages further on. For more than 30 years, England was repeatedly assaulted and ultimately some of the Vikings' victims preferred to pay them the bribe known as Danegeld —Danes' money—to stay away. This, of course, provided easy pickings and encouraged the Vikings to come more and more often to collect their cash.

This time, they looted the church so thoroughly that the caretaker monks abandoned the island. Before they left, they buried their treasure, leaving one lone monk to guard it. It seems that he was still there 19 years later, in 825CE, when the Vikings came back for a fourth time, and demanded that he tell them the whereabouts of the treasure. When he refused, he was butchered.

On this occasion, the Vikings may have left Iona empty-handed, but they knew there were lavish pickings elsewhere and inevitably, they returned again and again. Before long, the mere sight of a Viking warship approaching a coast was enough to create onshore panic and frantic efforts to escape. There was no escape. Once the Vikings were inside a town or village, there was only one outcome. They killed the inhabitants or seized them to sell as slaves. They looted homes and buildings, stripping them of food, clothing, tools, implements, and anything else they could find. Before they went back to their ships, they threw ignited torches onto the straw roofs of huts, sending columns of flame and smoke funneling into the sky.

Before long, the mere sight of a Viking warship approaching a coast was enough to create onshore panic and frantic efforts to escape. There was no escape.

VIKING CODE OF PRACTICE

Despite their ferocity, Viking pirates had their code of practice. They followed strict rules regarding the fair division of loot, and it was "not done" to attack a ship while it was being assaulted by other pirates. This was not unexpected from a society that rated honor and living by it as paramount social virtues. But this code did nothing, of course, to lessen the impact of Viking piracy and the damage it caused. Not just England suffered. The Vikings occupied islands off Scotland, destroyed the resident Picts and wiped out the established communities of the west coast, and similar calamities were repeated throughout Europe.

All over the continent, Danish and Norwegian Vikings inspired dread, bringing death and destruction. They marauded through France and Spain, where they attacked the port of Cadiz in 844CE. Moving on through Italy, they attacked the Balearic islands and crossed the Mediterranean to raid North Africa. To their shocked victims, it seemed as if the Vikings could go wherever and do whatever they wanted. Viking warships staged hit-and-run raids, grabbing loot, loading it onto their ships, and sailing away before their stunned victims could react.

One reason why all this became feasible was that the Vikings were superlative sailors. Their oarsmen achieved impressive speeds, up to a maximum of 15 knots (17 miles per hour/27.78km), and were able to make long journeys, not only in the open sea but along rivers. They sailed down the River Rhine and the River Elbe to plunder rich targets in Germany. Paris was attacked more than once by Vikings, who reached the French capital by navigating up the River Seine. Other Vikings headed up the River Rhône or penetrated deep into northeastern France along the River Loire, making for the fabulous booty to be found in the rich abbeys of the region. To the east, Swedish Vikings sailed the length of the great Russian rivers Volkhov, Dnieper, and Volga and later staged raids across the Caspian Sea. The Swedes also circumnavigated Europe, a feat made possible by the very shallow draft of Viking longships.

These were remarkable achievements, unique in their time, and therefore all the more frightening to people who had simply assumed that the "impossible" could not be done.

"It was not thought possible that they could have made such a voyage," said the scholar Alcuin in 793CE, when the Vikings sailed 400 miles (644km) across the North Sea in winter—with no landmarks to guide them—and sacked Lindisfarne. They understood the sea and could read its changing moods like no one else in their time. Not only could they navigate out of sight of land, they charted their destinations so accurately they were only about two percent off target at landfall compared to the reckonings of twenty-first-century satellites.

The Vikings were not just raiders, but also daring explorers. In 985CE, Erik the Red crossed the waters of the north Atlantic, sailing from the Viking colony on Iceland to icebound Greenland.

They could sail along any clear waterway, such as a river, lake, or channel, and so reach almost any destination, however remote. No one, it appears, was safe from them. The Vikings even sailed beyond the immediate boundaries of the world as they knew it, crossing the north Atlantic to land on Iceland and Greenland, as well as Labrador in present-day Canada.

SUPERIOR SEAMANSHIP

The seas that the Vikings crossed to reach such exotic destinations lay in the far northern latitudes of Europe, close to the Arctic icefields, which did not often provide calm waters or clear weather. Heavy sea mists, fog, rain, or thick overcasts could block out the sky and obscure the Sun or the stars, which the Vikings used as navigational aids. On such days, the Vikings used a "sun stone," made of Icelandic spar, to help locate the position of the Sun. Icelandic spar is a calcite mineral that is sensitive to light. When turned in the direction of the Sun, it changes color slightly. So, even beneath cloud and fog cover, the "sun stone" was still able to detect the Sun's location.

The superior seamanship of the Vikings enabled them to do more than raid, rob, enslave, and sail home. Unlike many other pirates, they were looking for land to seize and settle. Their wide-ranging pirate raids enabled the Vikings to view other parts of Europe and beyond, where the land was more fertile, the climate more clement, and the long-term prospects more feasible than they were in Scandinavia. Luxuriantly fertile England was a prime target, but it was by no means the only one. Ireland also had its attractions for the Norwegian Vikings. As a center of Christian art and learning, its churches and monasteries were a lucrative source of plunder, and with its lush green countryside Ireland was also a promising place to settle.

By the middle of the ninth century CE, the invaders had established coastal settlements in Limerick, Waterford, Wexford, Cork, and Arklow. At first, the Vikings used these bases as winter quarters for hit-and-run raids on the mainland, using the rivers of Ireland, notably the Shannon. Later, though, the coastal settlements became jumping-off grounds for campaigns further inland as well as the starting points for permanent settlement. The most important of these was the one planted in Dublin Bay in 852CE by the joint leaders Ivarr the Boneless, a Dane, and Olaf the White, the son of a Norwegian warlord. Olaf got

> The Vikings even sailed beyond the immediate boundaries of the world as they knew it, crossing the north Atlantic to land on Iceland, Greenland, and Labrador.

GUIDED BY POLARIS

Latitude sailing was another very effective Viking navigation method. It involved following the line of latitude on which their destination stood until they reached it. To make sure they maintained the right latitude at sea, the Vikings used a long notched stick, noting the length of the shadow cast by the stick on the deck. If the shadow was longer or shorter than it should have been, the Vikings altered course until the shadow was again of the proper length. At night, the Vikings steered by Polaris, the North Star, which helped them fix their north–south position at sea. The position of Polaris was regularly checked and the Vikings altered their course to keep the star in the right place in relation to their vessel.

the best of the deal, becoming king of Dublin in 853CE. Ivarr had to find fresh fields to conquer, but that did not prove difficult. Despite 60 years of regular raids on England, plenty of promising targets remained to be exploited. In 865CE, together with his brothers Halfdene and Hubba, Ivarr led the Great Heathen Army in the invasion East Anglia in eastern England. First, they headed north toward York, which was then the Anglo-Saxon city of Eoforwic. The Anglo-Saxons, unfortunately for them, were embroiled in a civil war at the time, so facilitating Ivarr's capture of their city, which was subsequently renamed Jorvik.

A terrifying sight: armed to the teeth, already wearing helmets and shields, Viking raiders pull on their oars as they approach the Irish coast with sail furled, bent on raiding, raping, plunder, and destruction.

To all intents and purposes, Ivarr was an unlikely conqueror. He was crippled by a bone disease that affected his legs and he had to be carried about on a shield. He could, however, ride a horse, which was how he traveled from East Anglia to York. Four years later, he proved that he did not lack the merciless temperament of the Vikings.

In 869CE, Ivarr the Boneless moved back to East Anglia, where he demanded that King Edmund, later St Edmund, submit to him as his vassal now that the Vikings had destroyed his army and killed his thegns. Edmund refused, telling Ivarr that as a Christian king, he would never become the vassal of a pagan. In a fury, Ivarr ordered that he should be bound and beaten with rods. *In his Life of St Edmund, King of East Anglia*, the monk-chronicler Abbo of Fleury described what happened next:

The impious one then…led the devout king to a firm living tree, and tied him there with strong bonds, and beat him with whips…. They then shot spears at him, as if it was a game, until he was entirely covered with their missiles, like the bristles of a hedgehog. When Ivarr the impious pirate saw that the noble king would not forsake Christ, he ordered Edmund beheaded…. The heathen dragged the holy man to his death, and with one stroke struck off his head.

Eight years later, the onslaughts of the Danish Vikings persuaded Alfred the Great, also known as the Anglo-Saxon king Alfred of Wessex (849–899CE), to compromise with them. An area in eastern England, roughly half of the country, came under Danelaw, where Viking laws and customs prevailed. Alfred's son, Edward the Elder (c.870–924CE), retrieved the Danelaw by 918CE but eventually, integration blurred the differences between Vikings and Anglo-Saxons. Generations on, their original identities lapsed and both began to regard themselves as "English."

The same process was at work in Scotland and also in Ireland, which was never to come under complete Viking domination. As settlement replaced piracy, the Viking raids ceased in around 950CE. The final showdown occurred on April 23, 1014, at the Battle on Clontarf. There, Irish forces led by Brian Boru, the High King, whose authority was recognized throughout most of Ireland, met Máel Mórda mac Murchada, King of Leinster, whose army was chiefly composed of Viking mercenaries from Dublin. After a ferocious struggle, which cost the lives of both commanders, the Irish finally prevailed. This brought an end to Viking power in Ireland, though their influence remained in the towns they had founded, the trade they had created, and the place-names they left behind.

THE BARBARY COAST

With the next upsurge of piracy, some four or five centuries later, the Mediterranean became the center of operations once again. The Barbary Coast along the shorelines of Libya, Algeria, Tunisia, and Morocco was turned into pirate country. This was no coincidence. The spark that relit the flame was the Crusading era, which began in 1095. At this time, Christians and Muslims violently contested possession of the Holy Land. Ultimately, the Muslims were victorious, but this was not the end of the matter. A fierce enmity, still apparent today, burned on and turned adherents of the two religions into traditional enemies. Long after the end of the Crusades in 1303, the battle was still being fought in another context, the sea, by Arab and also Berber pirates. The Berbers gave their name to the "Barbary Coast," which lay along the shorelines of Libya, Algeria, Tunisia, and Morocco in North Africa. Muslim ships and coasts were immune from the depredations of the Barbary pirates,

A Barbary ship at sea: the rowers, usually prisoners or slaves, were whipped to make them pull their oars faster.

In 1492, King Ferdinand II of Aragon (below) and his wife Queen Isabella I of Castile ejected from Spain the last of the former rulers, the Muslim Moors. Many Moors afterward became pirates.

as they came to be known, but it was always open season on Christians and other non-Muslim "infidels."

A further boost to piracy came after 1492, when the forces of the Catholic sovereigns King Ferdinand of Aragon (1452–1516) and Queen Isabella of Castile (1451–1504) ejected the last of the Muslim Moors, who had ruled in Spain for almost eight centuries. The Moors went into exile in the cities of the North African coast. Burning with the urge for revenge, they embarked on a series of "Jihad" (holy war) expeditions against Christian ships and communities. Their most coveted prizes were white European women, who could be sold to brothels.

Muslim women did not necessarily avoid this fate. In practice, Barbary pirates could be far less discriminating than the anti-infidel principle might suggest. The pirates were willing to seize and enslave anyone, Muslim or otherwise, particularly after they were able to leave the confines of the Mediterranean and, like the Vikings, range far beyond their home territory.

CONQUERING THE OPEN SEAS

Faraway operations overseas did not come about, however, until the seventeenth century, when the pirates adopted sailing ships that eclipsed their original vessels, the galleys. Galleys had been in use since ancient times, but were suitable only for waterways like the tideless, relatively calm Mediterranean Sea. They were mainly driven by men heaving on oars, although they also carried masts and sails to keep a ship out of trouble when it was becalmed or in danger of running aground or of spiking itself on rocky coasts. Although some superlative sailors, like the early Carthaginians, the Ancient Greeks, or, much later, the Vikings, ventured beyond the Pillars of Hercules (the Straits of Gibraltar) and into the ocean beyond, galleys were unsuited to the mighty Atlantic rollers and dangerous Atlantic currents, and their oarsmen were rendered utterly helpless before the mighty power of the high seas.

Sailing ships, however, made it possible to handle ocean conditions much more successfully, with the added bonus of broadside guns, which could be used to shatter an enemy's timbers. Once the Barbary pirates began to utilize these ships, their range of operations was greatly expanded. This is evident from the number of different of destinations where the Barbary pirates captured millions of slaves. Few coastal areas of Europe remained immune from the *razzias,* as the slaving voyages were known. Slaves were seized from the shores of Italy, Spain, Portugal, France, and England and Barbary pirates apparently ventured far beyond the continent to Iceland, which lay on the edge of the Arctic Circle.

Thousands of French, English, and Spanish ships were lost to the Barbary pirates, and the coasts they had raided were abandoned for safer homes inland. The pirate raids were so devastating that only in the nineteenth century were the vulnerable coasts populated once again. As for the pirates' slaving activities, it has been reckoned that up to 1,500,000 Christians from Europe alone were seized for sale in the slave markets of Morocco and Algeria.

The galleys used by the pirates of the Barbary coast were well suited to sailing in the tideless Mediterranean, but could not cope with the mighty rollers and powerful, dangerous currents of the Atlantic Ocean.

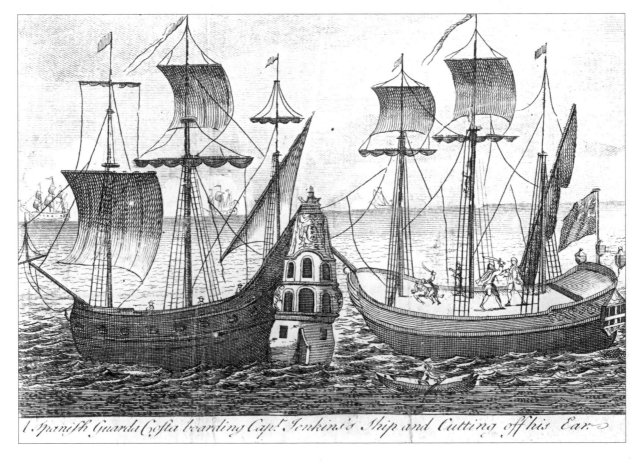

1 Spanish Guarda Costa boarding Capt. Jenkins's Ship and Cutting off his Ear.

Kair Ad Din, better known as Barbarossa or Red Beard, was the most famous and successful of a family of four pirate brothers. In one raid, on Naples in Italy, he captured 4000 prisoners.

In the sixteenth century, Algeria was the principal destination for these captured unfortunates after it was turned into the Mediterranean's major market for the sale of plunder or slaves by a family of four pirate brothers. They were Ishaq, Aruj, Ilyas, and the most famous of them and apparently the youngest, Khair ad Din (c.1480–1546), who was known to Europeans as Barbarossa or Red Beard.

THE RISE OF BARBAROSSA

Like his brothers, Barbarossa was born on the island of Midilla, later renamed Lesbos by the Greeks. Their mother, Katalina, was a Christian, and was, it seems, the widow of a priest before marrying their father, Yakup. At first, the brothers were employed as sailors, working to combat the privateering activities of the Knights of St John of Jerusalem, originally a crusading order but now based on the island of Rhodes. While returning in their father's ship from a trading mission to Tripoli in Lebanon, Aruj and his younger brother Ilyas were attacked by a vessel belonging to the Knights. Ilyas was killed, their father's ship captured, and Aruj, who lost his left arm in the fighting, was taken prisoner and incarcerated in the Knights' castle of Bodrum on Rhodes. Subsequently the lost limb was replaced with a prosthetic made of silver, earning Aruj the nickname of "Silver Arm." Aruj remained in prison for three years before Barbarossa discovered where he was and staged a daring rescue. Once free, Aruj headed for Italy and next moved on to Egypt. There, he presented himself before the Mameluke Sultan Qansoh al-Ghuri and persuaded him to hand over a ship so that he could attack Christian-ruled islands such as Rhodes, Malta, and Crete.

In about 1505, Aruj expanded his operations. He seized three ships and based himself on the island of Djerba off the Tunisian coast. From there, he was able to patrol the western Mediterranean and earned plaudits in the Islamic world by rescuing the Mudejars—the small number of Muslims still living in Christian Spain—and taking them to North Africa. Meanwhile, in 1511, the Spaniards captured Algiers. With

AN ALLEGIANCE OF PIRATES AND SULTANS

The Spaniards possessed a formidable army, one that might not be so easy to defeat. Barbarossa, who took Aruj's place as sole leader of the Algerines—as the pirates of Algiers were called—asked for aid from Selim Khan I, the Sultan of the Ottoman Turkish Empire (1467–1520). For the Sultan, who aimed to extend his Empire and make it the most powerful and influential of Muslim possessions, this request was a prize chance to gain the allegiance of a successful band of pirates. With that, he would acquire control over their principal pirate haunt in Algiers. He sent troops and ultimately, in 1529, the Spaniards were driven away. Sultan Selim, meanwhile, had died and in return for Ottoman aid, Barbarossa declared allegiance to his successor, Sultan Suleiman Khan I, (1494–1566), better known as Suleiman the Magnificent.

this, the Barbary pirates were faced with the loss of their prime base and Aruj and Barbarossa were called in to expel the Christian invaders. They managed to retrieve Algiers in 1516, but two years later Aruj died in a battle against the Spaniards as they attempted to win back the city.

In 1533, Suleiman appointed Barbarossa Admiral in Chief and furnished him with a great fleet, which, five years later, finished Spanish ambitions in the eastern Mediterranean and secured it for the Ottomans for the next 33 years. Eleven years later, in 1544, the King of France, Francis I, asked Suleiman for aid in fighting the Spaniards, who had declared war on him. Suleiman sent Barbarossa, who thrashed the Spaniards yet again and for good measure captured the Spanish-controlled port of Naples in Italy. But once a pirate, always a pirate, and during his raid on Naples, Barbarossa took 4000 prisoners. They were afterward sold into slavery together with another 9000 captives seized on the Lipari Islands—almost the entire population. Suleiman rewarded Barbarossa for his achievements by making him Supreme Commander of the Ottoman Navy in the Mediterranean with the title of *Beylerbey,* meaning Commander of Commanders. In 1545, Barbarossa retired to the palace he had built for himself close to the Bosphorus waterway in Istanbul, dying there the next year.

Like Barbarossa, several other Mediterranean pirates were appointed beylerbeys and acquired the title of *Reis* (admiral), which hid their activities behind a mask of legitimacy. Strictly speaking, the Reises were privateers, whose voyages were licensed by a recognized ruler. The deal was that the pirate ships were fitted out by rulers, aristocrats, merchants, and other wealthy men and commanded by the beylerbeys. They handed over 10 percent of the value of the plunder or the prices fetched in the market by the sale of slaves. In reality, whatever the beylerbeys were called made little difference. They were still pirates preying on shipping and coastal villages, inspiring terror at the mention of their names. Homes, property, freedom, and life itself were at their mercy, and their mercy was in very short supply.

For most of the sixteenth and seventeenth centuries, the beylerbeys were ruthless slavers. One of the most infamous was Turgut Reis (1485–1565), a friend of Barbarossa who succeeded him as Supreme Commander in the Mediterranean

Suleiman sent Barbarossa, who thrashed the Spaniards yet again, and for good measure captured the Spanish-controlled port of Naples in Italy.

Aruj, a brother of Barbarossa, whose pirate ship is shown here, was given the nickname of "Silver Arm" after he lost his left arm in battle. It was replaced with a prosthetic made of silver.

after Barbarossa's death in 1546. Turgut was nothing if not thorough. In 1551, he removed the entire population of Gozo, one of the Maltese islands in Mediterranean—up to 6000 people—and transported them to Libya for sale in the slave markets. Four years later, he appeared off Bastia on the island of Corsica, pillaged the town and carried off another 6000 prisoners for the same purpose. Another 4000 victims headed for the slave markets after Turgut Reis landed on the coast of Granada, in southern Spain, seized several coastal settlements, and enslaved yet another 4000 people.

INDISCRIMINATE ENSLAVEMENT

Meanwhile, other Barbary pirates had been just as busy. In 1554, their tally of victims amounted to 7000 after they assaulted Vieste in southern Italy. In 1558, the pirates pillaged Ciutadella on the Balearic island of Menorca, destroyed the town, butchered most of the inhabitants, and finally set sail for Istanbul with 3000 survivors on board. The Balearic islands were a favorite target of the Barbary pirates, and their frequent visits prompted the building of coastal watchtowers and fortified buildings. Even churches acquired their fortifications, but the beleaguered inhabitants of Formentera had no faith in such defenses and abandoned their island. It was a wise, if depressing, strategy. The Barbary pirates were not the least discriminating when it came to the class of candidates they enslaved. Anyone and everyone had their use, so anyone and everyone was susceptible when the pirates came calling. The rich, the eminent and others with suitable social connections were set aside for ransom. The poor were sold into slavery. Many of them were fated for the back-breaking labor of galley slavery; chained to the oars of pirate ships, they had minimal chances of survival. Those who were slightly luckier might be purchased in the slave market as domestic servants or gardeners. Those who were physically attractive might be bought for the harems of a Sultan's palace, where they lived out the rest of their lives in perfumed confines. Sometimes, prisoners could buy their freedom by converting to Islam, but for others, their first destinations were the prisons of Algiers, where, in the early seventeenth century, as many as 20,000 captives could be kept at one time.

Algiers, an overcrowded, overheated, beaten-up, squalid old town, became the beylerbeys' principal seat of government in 1587. They also controlled Tripoli and Tunisia, two other Barbary pirate territories, which were nominally attached to the Ottoman Empire. In 1659, however, the Ottoman *pashas* dispatched from Istanbul to rule these territories were sent packing by their subjects. The cities of Tripoli, Tunis, and Algeria now became independent pirate states, where anarchy prevailed and the main, often only, source of income was piracy and plunder.

Barbary piracy was, of course, a very lucrative pie and European adventurers wanted to get their fingers into it. For example, an Albanian known as Murat the Great turned pirate after he was captured by Barbary slavers in 1546. Murat became the first of the corsairs to take his sailing ship out into the Atlantic where he attacked and plundered the Canary Islands. Another European, who adopted the Barbary name of Murat and became an Ottoman beylerbey as Murat Reis, was a Dutchman born Jan Janszoon van Haarlem (*c*.1575–*c*.1641). Janszoon signed on as a merchant seamen in 1600, but later switched to privateering. In 1605, he sailed from the port of La Rochelle, on the Bay of Biscay, carrying letters of marque from the Dutch authorities to capture Spanish pirates operating out of their base at Dunkirk in northern France.

At this time, the Dutch had been at war with Spain since 1583, but it seems that they had exhausted each other by 1609, when a truce between them was declared. The truce was to last for 12 years, but this was too long for Janszoon and other privateers who had enjoyed the benefits of booty for some time and wanted more. They now resorted to piracy, which was just as profitable—and exciting— though it lacked the protection afforded privateers by their employers.

Janszoon the pirate was at large for nine years before Barbary corsairs captured him during a raid on Lanzerote in the Canary Islands. The corsairs took him to Algiers, where Janszoon saw for himself the vast value in goods and slaves that passed through the markets of this thriving trade center. At any one time, Algiers contained some 20,000 captives for sale in the slave markets and Janszoon was impressed. Algiers was undoubtedly the place to be and corsair company yielded the best connections. In 1618, he therefore joined the corsairs and promptly set out to sea, sailing as quartermaster to another Dutchman-turned-pirate, Sulayman Reis, whose original surname was Van Veenboer. Sulayman, the admiral of the Algerian pirate fleet, retired the following year and Janszoon, now Murat Reis, took over his ships.

During his career, Sulayman Reis did not forget his Dutch origins and

At any one time, Algiers contained some 20,000 captives for sale in the slave markets.

After Barbarossa's death in 1546, the privateer and Ottoman admiral Turgut Reis succeeded him as Supreme Commander in the Mediterranean. Later, Turgut was appointed Bey of Algiers.

Millions of slaves were sold at the slave market at Algiers over the centuries it lasted. This illustration was made in 1684, but the sale of slaves was still going on in the early twentieth century.

when he went pirating, he was sure to identify and protect Dutch ships and their crews. Murat Reis had no such scruples. As far as he was concerned, any non-Barbary ship encountered at sea was fair game.

Murat Reis soon discovered that loot and booty were not the only advantages of piracy—there were also several political plums going. In 1619, peace was signed between Algiers and France and several other European nations. Piracy was discontinued, and Murat Reis returned to his family's home at Salé in Morocco. Shortly afterward, though, Salé became a semi-independent pirate state and a base for the Salé pirates. Murat Reis was elected Admiral and president of Salé city. He had already prepared to resume operations by building a fleet of 17 fast ships and in 1622, the year he converted to Islam, he went a-pirating once again.

Running up the Moroccan flag on his masthead, he claimed diplomatic immunity from attack and sailed in November 1622 for the Dutch port of Veere, in Zeeland, where he wanted his ship repaired. While in harbor at Veere, Murat Reis was joined by a number of Dutch sailors, despite strong protests from the Netherlands government. Officials arrived at the docks in Veere with Murat's wife and children in tow to persuade him to go home to Salé, but the pirate refused to budge.

If his new recruits were looking for adventure, danger, and loot, these were not long in coming. Once the repairs to his ships were completed and the time came to leave Veere, the first thing Murat did was to attack several French vessels. The next was to fight off an attack on Salé, when it was besieged in 1623 by the Moroccan Sultan Moulay Ziden en Nasir (1555–1627). Much to the Sultan's dismay, his forces were repulsed and he was reduced to covering up this disgrace by appointing Murat Reis as Governor of Salé. In 1624, the humiliated Sultan gave Murat his daughter as his third wife, though in Islamic society she was considered as only his second since the first wife was Christian.

MURAT'S REYKJAVIK RAID

Arguably, the most unusual expedition staged in 1627 by Murat Reis was his raid on Reykjavik, Iceland, and the nearby Westman islands. Wet, windy, changeable, and subject to eruptions from more than 100 volcanoes, Iceland could hardly have been more different from the heat and lushness of the Mediterranean. Murat Reis had obviously done his homework thoroughly, because the raid took place at a most favorable time of year in Iceland, between July 4 and 19, when these far north latitudes enjoyed round-the-clock daylight. Murat hired a Danish pilot, possibly captured in a previous raid and afterward sold as a slave. The pilot guided the three pirate ships out into the Atlantic and around western Europe until they reached their destination far to the north.

Reykjavik, the Icelandic capital, was something of a disappointment. It seems that the ship attacked by the pirates in the harbor yielded only some salt fish and animal hides. The pirates moved on to towns on the south coast. In one of them, Grindavík, the inhabitants were able to run away across the lava fields and hide

In 1683, Barbary corsairs returned the French consul at Algiers to his ship by cannon—an incidence of great notoriety at the time.

Steven Decatur was a great American seafaring hero. In 1804, he led a commando raid on Tripoli, Libya to set fire to the grounded USS *Philadelphia* and so deny the vessel to the Barbary pirates.

until the attackers went away, but the people of Heimaey, which was remote and secluded, were not so fortunate. The pirates killed some 30 people there, and carried off another 400 as slaves. Then they burnt down the church and the local warehouse. Most of the captives were never seen again, but 27 were ransomed in 1637 and returned to Iceland. One returnee, a woman called Guríur Símonardóttir, who was seized from her home in Heimaey, bought her own way back from the slave market in Algiers to Iceland through Tunisia, Italy, and Denmark. The "Turkish Raid," as it was termed, made a profound impression in Iceland. Soon after it took place, a law was passed which stated that any Turk found in Iceland must be killed on sight. No Turk ever met this fate, but almost 350 years passed before the law was repealed.

THE SACK OF BALTIMORE

Murat's next recorded pirate venture took place four years after the "Turkish Raid" at Baltimore in Cork, Ireland. The pirate ships descended on this small coastal village in 1631 and few villagers escaped capture. The rest were taken away to meet various fates. In his poem "The Sack of Baltimore," Thomas Davis (1814–45), the Irish poet-politician wrote:

"Oh! Some must tug the galley's oar, and some must tend the steed;
This boy will bear the Sheik's chibook [tobacco pipe] and that a Bey's jerreed [javelin]
Oh! Some are in the arsenal, by beauteous Dardanelles;
And some are in the caravan to Mecca's sandy dells.

The maid that Bandon gallant sought is chosen for the Dey;
She's safe—he's dead—she stabbed in the Midst of his serai [palace]
And when to die a death of fire, that noble maid they bore,
She only smiled—O'Driscoll's child—she thought of Baltimore."

Murat Reis did moderately well out of the Baltimore raid. He returned to Algiers with 108 captives for sale in the slave market. In 1635, however, he was taken prisoner by the Knights of St John of Jerusalem, who by this time had moved from Rhodes to

Malta. He escaped after five years in confinement. Now in his mid-sixties, Murat decided it was time to retire from active piracy and turned instead to desk jobs in Morocco. He became Governor of Oualidia in the south and afterward, Governor of the Castle of Maladia on the west coast. He disappears from the record, presumed dead, in 1641.

The long and successful careers of beylerbeys like Murat Reis were made possible by several factors. First, in the sixteenth and seventeenth centuries, there was no dominant state, like the Roman Empire, to rid the Mediterranean of piracy or at least lessen its impact. The only power of appreciable size, the Ottoman Turkish Empire, was actually in collusion with the pirates.

Second, any organized opposition to the pirates was weakened by those nations that paid them "blood money" in exchange for immunity from attack. There were some attempts to control the pirate menace, but they were minimal compared to the stranglehold imposed by the threats and intimidation of pirates and privateers and the profound dread they inspired. Efforts against these renegades by the Republic of Venice or the Knights of St John barely scratched the surface of the problem. Even Admiral Michiel de Ruyter (1607–1676), the Netherlands' most brilliant and renowned naval commander, was not entirely successful when he hunted for Dutch pirates who preyed on Dutch shipping between 1637 and 1640. More often, the only hope lay in the efforts of religious orders, such as the Congregation of the Mission based in Paris, or the Trinitarians, a special order of monks, whose task it was to retrieve captives from slavery. They were frequently funded by legacies donated for this specific purpose from all over Europe.

Then a newcomer with a much more pugnacious attitude entered the fray. In 1784, Moroccan pirates seized the first ship belonging to the nascent United States, which had won its independence from Britain only a year before. The same year, two more ships—the *Maria* of Boston and the *Dauphin* of Philadelphia—were plundered by Algerines and their crews taken ashore and

Efforts against these renegades by the Republic of Venice or the Knights of St John barely scratched the surface of the problem.

PIRACY AS FOREIGN POLICY

A factor, and possibly the most influential one, that allowed piracy to flourish was the cynical use made of the pirates by the great powers of Europe. The French, for instance, positively encouraged the pirates to attack Spanish targets as part of their longstanding rivalry with Spain. Subsequently, piracy became an ingredient of English and Dutch foreign policy against France. At other times, European powers paid lip service to the challenge without seriously damaging the pirates' prospects. In 1655, for instance, the republican government of England sent Admiral Robert Blake (1599–1657) to give Tunisian pirates a thorough thrashing. In 1682–3, a French fleet bombarded Algiers. The Algerines responded by tying the French consul to a gun and blowing him to pieces. These were only two of numerous expeditions ostensibly designed to finish the pirate threat once and for all, but they were really charades. Not one of them backed up the initial attack with any vigor or looked as if they were seriously addressing the pirate problem.

PUNITIVE EXPEDITIONS

At the Congress of Vienna, which brought the Napoleonic Wars to an end in 1815, Europe got tough. Steps were taken to suppress the slave trade, already abolished by Britain in 1807, thereby cutting off the Barbary pirates' principal source of revenue. Punitive expeditions by the British and the Dutch to bombard Algiers succeeded in terrifying the inhabitants and prompted the pirate state of Tunis into surrendering more than 3000 prisoners. All this seriously damaged the once fearsome reputation of the Barbary pirates and drastically reduced the tribute and the ransom money they had been accustomed to receive.

President Washington authorized the creation of the US Navy and the construction of the first six frigates, a type of armor-clad warship that was the most powerful afloat at the time.

put to work building fortifications. At first, the Americans responded by playing safe: when sailing the Atlantic, US ships attached themselves to foreign fleets whose countries had already bribed the pirates not to attack. Even so, ships were still being seized, Americans enslaved and thousands of dollars worth of goods stolen and sold.

THE CREATION OF THE UNITED STATES NAVY

By 1793, some 12 American ships had been captured. At last, the US Congress decided that tougher and more meaningful action was in order, requiring an armed American presence in the Mediterranean and other trouble spots. On March 27, 1794, US President George Washington (1732–99) authorized the creation of the United States Navy and the construction of the first six frigates, a type of armor-clad warship that was the most powerful afloat at the time.

By an armed presence, the Americans meant not only patrols or occasional intervention at the scene of pirate attacks, but a force capable of making war. Indeed, war followed in 1801 after the newly elected US president, Thomas Jefferson (1743–1826), refused to hand over $225,000 demanded by Yussif Karamanli, the pasha of Tripoli. Instead, Jefferson dispatched frigates to protect American interests in the Mediterranean and also, in 1803, ordered blockades of the Barbary coast accompanied by a series of raids on the Barbary cities. The pirates succeeded in capturing one of the US frigates, the *Philadelphia,* after it ran aground while patrolling the harbor at Tripoli. Four months later, in February 1804, a daring commando raid led by Stephen Decatur Jr (1779–1820) defied the defenders' 141 guns and denied the prize to the pirates by setting the *Philadelphia* on fire.

By 1805, after four years, Yussuf Karamanli was finally worn down and ended hostilities on June 10. Although the Americans had demonstrated their grit and muscle, the Barbary coast pirates were not yet completely tamed. American operations against them were temporarily interrupted by the War of 1812 with Britain, but 1815, the year after the war ended, saw the US Fleet back in the Mediterranean. This time, with the Second Barbary War, the hostilities were both brief and decisive. On March 3, the US Congress authorized a force of 10 vessels to sail for the Mediterranean. Four months later, after capturing two Algerine ships, including their flagship *Meshuda*, Commander Stephen Decatur Jr was in Algiers bully-bouncing the pirate ruler, the Dey, into surrender. The Dey went down in a fury of demands for tribute and threats of destruction, but in the end, he signed a treaty that included, most importantly, full shipping rights for American vessels and an end to the payment of tribute.

The triumph of a novice nation, a comparative pipsqueak in world terms, seemed to act as a catalyst for the long-established countries of Europe. Fear was replaced by anger at the pirate's insolence. The justification for paying out millions in bribes to keep the pirates away began to look shameful now that the United States had shown the honorable way to deal with them.

The Europeans, notably Britain and France, did much more than make the Mediterranean perilous for pirates. They were increasingly interested in colonizing the "Dark Continent" of Africa, and the French had plans to plant large numbers of settlers in Algeria, then part of the Ottoman Turkish Empire. To implement this, the French found a pretext for war in a dispute over payment for a consignment of wheat and in 1830, French forces marched into Algiers. This show of power was enough to panic the Dey of Algiers into instant surrender, and he went into exile. This act of craven submission in what was once the stronghold of Mediterranean piracy spelled the end for the Barbary pirates.

France ruled Algeria for the next 132 years and, after 1865, annexed the Barbary Coast itself. With the British already established on Gibraltar (1704) and Malta (1814), the imperial powers of Europe closed in so effectively that there was nowhere for the Barbary, or any other, pirates to go.

In 1830, when French forces marched into Algiers its ruler, the Dey, surrendered immediately. This cowardly response saw the end of the Barbary pirates not only in Algiers but right right along the Barbary Coast.

chapter 3

PIRATES OF THE FAR EAST

Piracy thrives when governments are weak. A feeble government facing difficult challenges at home or abroad, or preoccupied with maintaining a precarious hold on power, encourages pirates to do their worst and do it often. Civil wars and other internal disturbances or shifts of power that break down law, order, and, with that, security, also enable pirates to flourish unhindered.

The pattern was similar in Asia, where feudal Japan was the target of four viciously aggressive raids by Korean pirates in the ninth century. At this juncture, Japanese emperors were confronted with so much rebellion and crime that they formed a special defense force to deal with it. This was the beginning of the renowned *samurai* warrior caste, who were to dominate Japan for the next thousand years. At their inception, the samurai policed areas in which the Korean pirates appeared. The samurai inflicted so many casualties on the Koreans that they finally gave up and went back to Korea.

The samurai also tackled their own, home grown pirates, the *kaizoku,* or "sea robbers." Like the Koreans, the kaizoku attacked boats carrying rich cargo, notably the rice tax or shipments of grain, and were not above murdering their victims for loot. Their main theater of operations, the Inland Sea between the Japanese islands of Honshu, Shikoku,

A Chinese two-masted junk. Originally developed during the Han dynasty, the junk was one of the most successful ships in history, suited to war, trade, and exploration.

and Kyushu, formed an ideal setting for kaizoku raids. With their hundreds of islands, inlets, and coves, the coasts of the Inland Sea provided shelter and hiding places—the ideal setting from which to ambush trading ships and any other lucrative traffic sailing by. Other vantage points for pirates were provided by the Sandanbeki cliffs at Shirihama, a huge slab of rock 164ft (50m) high, on the southern coast of Honshu. Here, the pirates were reputed to live in a deep cave eroded out of the rock face, where they concealed their illicit treasure.

The imperial court finally took action to counter the danger piracy presented to peace, property, law, and order. In 931CE, for example, the court issued a decree that the roads and rivers between the eastern end of the Inland Sea, and the area around Kyoto and Nara on Honshu island, should be closely guarded to protect its palaces, its temples, and their treasures. Nara in particular had all the makings of a prize destination for pirates. Its temples were stuffed with tempting valuables. One of them, the Todai temple, contained more than 9000 items, all of them priceless, including the Great Buddha, a seated statue carved in bronze and 49ft (15m) high. Still, Nara remained vulnerable even after the decree of 931CE. No positive action had been taken despite the decree, and the order had to be repeated in each of the next two years. Finally, in 932CE, a new post was created for a pirate-hunter. Grandly named *tsuibu haizoku shi* (ambassador for the pursuit and capture of pirates), it is unknown whether or not he actually did anything. In any event, the "ambassador" was unable to prevent an impudent pirate assault in 934CE, during which a government granary in Iyo province on Shikoku island was set on fire and burned to the ground.

FUJIWARA SUMITOMO REVOLT

Two years after the granary was destroyed, the imperial court was faced with a well-organized pirate revolt led by an aristocrat, Fujiwara Sumitomo (died 941CE), who had put together his own kaizoku group. Sumitomo was a native of Iyo province and was first employed by the Japanese military to hunt down and destroy pirates. But by 936CE he had clearly undergone a change of heart—and a change of employment—to become a pirate himself. He mounted plundering raids in style and in strength with a fleet numbering around 1000 vessels. However, he lost his men at a significant rate when a new governor of Iyo province offered them a tempting deal to renounce piracy. Some 30 pirate chiefs co-operated with the governor, offering him lists of

The Great Buddha in the Todai temple at Nara on Honshu, Japan. Rows of statues of the Buddha often appear in Buddhist temples in Asia, but this is one of the greatest and most valuable.

candidates. Ultimately, more than 2500 men gave themselves up, confessed their sins and received pardons. They were given land, clothes, food, and a supply of seed and were told to become farmers.

This plan was all very well in theory, and more easily said than done. At this time in Japan, the prospects were hardly favorable for taking up an agricultural lifestyle. Disease and famine were rife in 936CE, and the years that followed were even more disastrous. Predictably, the penitents soon reneged and returned to their old ways. In 938 and 939CE, Sumitomo was back in harness, once more leading pirate raids and making a great success of it. He controlled almost all the traffic in the Inland Sea and had supporters in the capital, Nara. These proved their usefulness when Fujiwara was summoned before the Emperor Yutaakira (died 967CE). While the emperor was demanding that Sumitomo explain himself, Sumitomo's supporters staged a timely diversion by setting fire to some of the imperial buildings.

Nara, which stands among picturesque wooded hills, was Japan's first capital city between 709BCE and 84BCE. The city was, and still is, famous for its annual display of cherry blossom.

Taira Masakado, a samurai and pirate who led a rebellion against the Japanese Emperor Yutaakira and proclaimed himself Shinno, which meant "new emperor."

Sumitomo, it appears, was not punished for his misdemeanors. Instead, he was set free. He was certainly not cured of his proclivity for piracy and initiated a plan to attack Kyoto. The vice-governor of Bizen province, Fujiwara Kokoda, somehow learned of the plan and set out for Kyoto to alert the emperor. He never got there. Sumitomo was waiting for him at a post station, together with a number of his men, who showered him and his family with arrows. Kokoda was taken prisoner and his ears cut off. His nose was sliced in two, his wife kidnapped, and his children murdered. Not long afterward, Sumitomo assaulted Bitchu province, close by the Inland Sea, in western Honshu. At around the same time, dire news reached the Emperor Yutaakira (died 946CE) from northern Japan: a rebellion had broken out, led by the samurai Taira Masakado (died 940CE), who declared himself Shinno or "new Emperor." The rebellion was soon suppressed. Masakado was killed in battle and decapitated. Meanwhile, the Emperor played for time until his forces were free to deal with Fujiwara. As a lure, and to lull him into a false sense of complacency, Sumitomo was offered a highly ranked position at the imperial court. News of this prestigious appointment took some time to reach him. When it did, Sumitomo was flattered. Apparently not suspecting anything untoward, he gladly accepted the honor, but did not allow this to prevent him from further pirating. He put together a fleet of 400 ships and attacked Sanuki province on the island of Shikoku. Then, in 940CE, he embarked on a fresh series of raids, assaulting Dazaifu on the island of Kyushu, and then moving on to Suo province, on Honshu, where he burned down a government mint. This was almost the end of Sumitomo's pirate career. In 941CE, he managed to escape an attack by government forces, but he was finally brought to

battle in Hakata Bay, off the island of Kyushu where he met catastrophe. He lost 800 of his ships and many hundreds of his men, some of whom committed suicide by throwing themselves overboard when defeat seemed certain. Remarkably, Sumitomo escaped again, but was captured on his home ground in Iyo province four weeks later. His head was cut off and put on display in Kyoto.

LIFE ON THE EDGE

The sheer size of Fujiwara Sumitomo's forces, which included numerous pirate groups banded together, points to a sad reality that existed in tenth-century Japan and for a long time afterward. Pirates and would-be pirates had nothing to lose but their desperation when the balance of life was so fragile and there were so many potential perils to make it so. Disease was always there, ready to strike. Famine was a regular threat. Bad harvests could occur at any time and when they did, their effect was disastrous. There was always the chance that war, civil unrest, or the upheavals created by local warlords and their rivalries would upset the fragile equilibrium of everyday existence. Beggars on the streets of Japanese cities were a common sight, and so were corpses. Even the climate was inimical. It could lash Japan with destructive typhoons or threaten survival itself with the earthquakes and eruptions caused by the mass of volcanoes that thickly covered the map of the Japanese islands.

This was life on the edge, offering meager pickings at the best of times. The land barely yielded a living for many farmers or the sea for many fishermen. In these circumstances, it was unsurprising that large numbers of pirates came from the poorer regions of Japan, or from small islands and remote coastal villages where the inhabitants were all too familiar with privation. For many Japanese, piracy was the only way out. They had no choice but to accept the risk of facing savage punishments if they were seized by the formidable samurai.

Sumitomo was waiting for him at a post station together with a number of his men. Kokoda was taken prisoner and his ears cut off. His nose was sliced in two, his wife kidnapped, and his children murdered.

SAMURAI COLLECT SEVERED PIRATE HEADS

The samurai had come a long way since their inception, evolving into a force that typified military prowess and followed a strict code of conduct, known as *Bushido* (Way of the Warrior), which promised loyalty to the "divine" Japanese emperor, and their aristocratic masters, even to the death. Of these masters, the most eminent noble family was the Taira, who excelled as principal pirate-hunters to the emperor. In the early twelfth century, they policed the Inland Sea with devastating efficiency. In 1119, Taira Masamori selected 100 of his best men and embarked on an expedition that saw him return home by the end of the year with an impressively large number of severed pirate heads. Masamori's son, Taira Tadomori (1096–1153), set out to follow in his father's footsteps. Tadomori, however, was a slippery customer, not above setting aside samurai honor if it meant achieving his own nefarious ends. During an expedition of 1135, he attempted to increase his reward for the number of pirates captured by inflating his tally of 70 prisoners taken to include around 40 common criminals.

THE WOKOU PIRATES

The *wokou* made their first appearance in the records in 1223. That year, they struck at Korea from their bases on the northern coast of Kyushu and the islands of Iki and Tsushima. The wokou returned in 1226, when the Koreans, forewarned by previous experience, were able to field sufficient forces to capture all of the pirates. This time, "several tens of ships" were involved, compared with only two the previous year, and the pirates included numerous *ronin*. Experienced corsairs from the island of Tsushima, which was soon to become a major base for the wokou, acted as pilots.

Tadomori worked the system in several other ways, too. He forged a decree, purportedly issued by the emperor himself, which bestowed trading concessions on him. His commercial dealings with China linked him to smugglers plying the Inland Sea, which was under the control of the Taira clan. Tadomori also saw to it that the guards he placed to watch out for smugglers knew to turn a blind eye when required.

The Taira clan's role as pirate-hunters to the Japanese emperors ended violently in 1185, more than 30 years after Tadomori's death, when their rivals, the Minamoto, crushed them in a naval battle in the Inland Sea. Afterward, Yoritomo, head of the Minamoto clan, became the first Shogun (military dictator). The emperor, though retaining his divine status, became a figurehead, whose principal, if not only, occupation was writing poetry. In 1192, Minamoto relocated the capital city of Japan to Kamakura in central Honshu. This meant that the shogunate was further away from the former capital, Kyoto, and so even more distant from the seedbed of piracy among the small islands, coves, and inlets sited in the west. It turned out to be a call to arms for the pirates of the region, who had never been fully domesticated and needed little incentive to revive their operations.

The weapons of the wokou (*see* box above) spread terror and mayhem, in particular the deadly samurai sword, which was honed to maximum sharpness. Some wokou carried a sword in each hand. Spears, tridents, bows, and arrows also featured in wokou raids—as did guns after 1542, when the Portuguese introduced them. But even without guns, the wokou assault of 1226 still managed to wreak fearful violence on the Korean mainland, "destroying people and houses and looting valuables," especially "silver articles," according to a Korean chronicler. But despite wokou rapacity, Korean resistance was so ferocious that "half (the pirates) were killed or wounded." The wokou attempted to make a quick getaway, but were intercepted by Korean ships. Two wokou were captured and beheaded, but the rest managed to get away in the dark.

Despite this disconcerting experience, the wokou were willing to try again. They were spurred on by the destruction of the rice crop in Hizen province in Kyushu when a fierce typhoon tore across Kyushu and its adjacent islands in the autumn of 1226. Faced yet again with famine, the wokou resolved to make good the damage with another raid on Korea. But the assaults that followed in 1227 met with almost total disaster. The Koreans once more awaited the pirates in

The Japanese were obviously feeling diplomatic, and as a result, 90 pirates were executed in front of envoys who had come from Korea especially to witness their dispatch.

strength. They captured two wokou ships and decapitated more than 30 pirates. Other wokou who managed to get ashore and into the mountains were trapped in an ambush and killed. The Koreans made vociferous protests about the raid to the authorities in Kyushu. The Japanese were obviously feeling diplomatic and, as a result, 90 pirates were executed in front of envoys who had come from Korea especially to witness their dispatch.

THE KUSANO

After the mass executions, the pirates laid low for a while, until 1232, a year that followed more typhoons that had created further devastation and want on Kyushu. At this point, a new class of pirate entered the ring. These were junior members of the Kusano, a powerful samurai family from Karatsu on Kyushu Island, who raided Korea toward the end of 1232. Their favored samurai status may have saved them from the death sentence, for no executions followed. This, though, did not mean that Hojo Yasutoki (1183–1242), the *shikken* (regent) to the Minamoto shogunate, meant to let the matter go unavenged. Yasutoki was firmly against piracy, but instead of wiping it out by violent means, he preferred to co-operate with the Koreans to keep piracy under control. This friendlier approach persisted until the middle of the thirteenth century, when famines affecting Korea and, quite probably, Japan as well, struck yet again. To compound these disasters, the Mongols stepped up their attacks on Korea with a fresh incursion in 1253.

Co-operation had already begun to break down two years earlier when the Koreans started building fortifications designed to keep out Japanese pirates. The wokou returned nevertheless, in 1259, following another four years of famine that had ravaged both Korea and Japan. The wokou attacked yet again in 1263 and 1265, by which time Korea was in no fit state to put up effective resistance: the country was being absorbed by the Mongols, who completed their takeover in 1273.

A Japanese samurai, with his two swords. Although the samurai belonged to an elite caste, separate from ordinary Japanese society, their code of *Bushido* influenced the Japanese mindset until the late nineteenth century.

This was a fearful development for the Japanese. The Mongol leader, Kublai Khan (1219–1294), had made himself the first emperor of the Yuan Dynasty of China in 1271 but, not content with the vast expanses of China itself, sought to extend his power far beyond its borders to encompass, by 1279, the 12.75 million square miles (33 million square km) of territory that stretched from the Yellow to the Caspian Sea. In this vast sweep of territory, the subjects of Kublai Khan numbered around 100 million people, but the Japanese were not among them. Kublai made two attempts to invade Japan, and quite probably, fresh territorial gain was not his only motive. Now that Korea was part of his empire, it was likely that the ravages carried out by the wokou pirates over the last 50 years or so were also on his mind.

The samurai Minamoto Yoritomo (1147–1199). Descended from the Japanese imperial family, Yoritomo made himself the first shogun in 1192. The Minamoto shogunate lasted for some 140 years until it collapsed in 1333.

KUBLAI'S FIRST INVASION

Kublai's first invasion of Japan took place on October 3, 1274. The odds seemed decidedly against the Japanese forces, which included seasoned wokou and Matsuura pirates from the island province of Kyushu in the far south. Now occupying the unusual role of homeland defenders, they were among 10,000 Japanese troops facing four times that number fighting for Kublai Khan. Some

5000 of Kublai's soldiers came from the Korean vassal state of Koryo and his fleet of 900 ships was manned by some 6700 Koryo seamen. Using advanced weaponry, in the form of exploding bombs, gunpowder cannon, and poisoned arrows, Kublai's army initially appeared to be bludgeoning its way to a quick victory. The wokou and other Japanese defenders were finally cornered at Dazaifu on Kyushu. There, the Japanese awaited the arrival of the enemy, but to their surprise and relief, the enemy never appeared. Instead, after three weeks' hard fighting, the forces of Kublai Khan withdrew to their ships to rest and re-equip. This was where a powerfully destructive typhoon caught them and smashed them to pieces. Some 13,000 Mongols died and their invasion fleet was so thoroughly wrecked that Kublai was obliged to give up and go home.

The Japanese did not fool themselves that this was the end of Kublai Khan's assaults on their island country. But they took full advantage of their lucky escape to prepare themselves for the next invasion. Coastguards were posted along the shores opposite Korea to watch out for another Mongol fleet. A stone barrier, 6ft (2m) high and 12 miles (20km) long, backed by an earth embankment at the rear, was erected around Hakata Bay in 1275–76. Another Japanese defense was psychological. The wokou pirate raids of previous years had helped to create a terrifying image of the Japanese as a cruel and bloodthirsty people, living in a country of thieving thugs. The Japanese exploited this odious description to show Kublai Khan that their country could not be invaded with impunity. To this end, they refused point blank to yield to the demand that they recognize Kublai Khan as their suzerain, and

Kamakura was the chief base of the Minamoto shoguns. It became the capital city of Japan in 1192 and remained so until 1333, when the Hojo imperial dynasty came to an end.

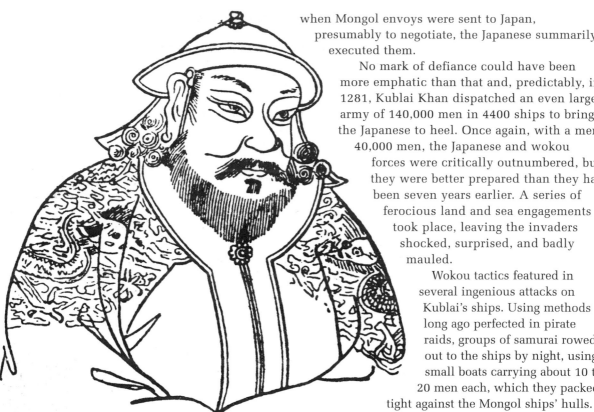

Kublai Khan made himself first emperor of the Yuan dynasty of China, but wanted to extend his power beyond even that huge country. Twice, in 1274 and 1281, Kublai tried, but failed, to conquer Japan.

when Mongol envoys were sent to Japan, presumably to negotiate, the Japanese summarily executed them.

No mark of defiance could have been more emphatic than that and, predictably, in 1281, Kublai Khan dispatched an even larger army of 140,000 men in 4400 ships to bring the Japanese to heel. Once again, with a mere 40,000 men, the Japanese and wokou forces were critically outnumbered, but they were better prepared than they had been seven years earlier. A series of ferocious land and sea engagements took place, leaving the invaders shocked, surprised, and badly mauled.

Wokou tactics featured in several ingenious attacks on Kublai's ships. Using methods long ago perfected in pirate raids, groups of samurai rowed out to the ships by night, using small boats carrying about 10 to 20 men each, which they packed tight against the Mongol ships' hulls. This strategy "crowded" the invaders' ships and stopped them from creating a beachhead onshore. In another type of attack, also carried out by night, 30 samurai swam out to a Mongol ship, leapt on board and after a short, sharp engagement beheaded the entire crew. Hand-to-hand fighting, in the preferred samurai style, also took place and one samurai, Kusano Jiro, maneuvered his ship alongside a Mongol vessel in broad daylight. He lost an arm in the fierce fighting that followed. Even so, Kusano managed to set the Mongol ship alight before escaping.

The Mongols tried to keep the samurai at bay by stretching chains between their ships and hurling stones into them in the hope of sinking the small boats they were using. Eventually the fight-back proved too much for the Japanese. A second Mongol fleet apparently numbering 3500 ships was due to arrive in Japanese waters, and the remnants of the first withdrew to Iki Island to wait for them. When they finally appeared, the Mongols inevitably turned the balance of the struggle in their own favor.

RESCUED BY DIVINE WIND

After a battle off Takashima on Hokkaido, the weight of numbers told and the Japanese were forced back. This enabled the Mongols to attack Hataka Bay, where they hoped to find fresh supplies to refurbish their own flagging stores. Then, without warning, capricious fate intervened once more. The Mongol fleet was still at anchor in the Hataka Bay when a typhoon, even more powerful than its predecessor of 1274, came howling in among the ships, destroying some two-thirds of them, killing thousands and leaving those who managed to survive to the dubious mercy of the vengeful Japanese. Few, it appears, survived to make the journey home. Among the Japanese, the typhoon of 1281, which undoubtedly saved Japan from Mongol rule, is still known as *kamikaze* (divine wind).

While the wokou were kept occupied in the defense of Japan, the Kamakura shogunate were able to keep their acts of piracy under better control, which increased the authority of the shogunate on Kyushu. The shoguns also kept the Strait of Korea and the adjacent territory under surveillance for a long time after the divine wind came to the rescue. Nevertheless, tension remained. The troops stationed along the coastline facing Korea did not stand down until 1320, some 40 years after the defeat of the Mongols. The power of Kublai Khan had declined since the disaster of 1281, but then so did the ability of the Hojo family (the hereditary regents or chief ministers to the shoguns) to keep the peace. After 125 years as the real rulers of Japan, the Hojo lost power in 1333. Yet again, Japan descended into the abyss of civil war.

Bad harvests, famine, and the desperation of a populace hard-pressed by poverty and want had already set the stage for a renewal of piracy. If anything, piracy now reached new heights of looting, slavery, intimidation, and chaos. A number of pirates were caught and beheaded from time to time, which appeared to dampen their activities for a while. But soon it was back to square one again as

Kublai's invasions of Japan were thwarted by typhoons that wrecked his ships and killed thousands of his men. Japan was saved, and afterward the Japanese called the typhoons *kamikaze*, meaning "divine wind."

conditions worsened and the old pressures took their toll. The wokou resumed raiding in 1350, when they staged six major raids on Korea. At this time, the Mongols' control over their Korean vassals was beginning to weaken, and it vanished entirely after the last of the Mongols departed in 1364.

Once again, it was open season on Korea and in the next 20 years, there were some 125 incursions into the peninsula. In 1384 alone, wokou raids on Korea averaged 40 a year. These were no mere hit-and-run strikes confined to the coastal towns and villages. They were highly organized campaigns aimed at carefully selected targets, the most common of them being the ships that took rice tax to the then capital city, Kaesong. The Koreans attempted to frustrate the pirates by switching to land transport, but the pirates were soon on to it. They sailed up both coasts of the Korean peninsula until they were within reach of the storehouses sited inland, then disembarked and struck into the interior to raid them. Not only that, the wakou captured local inhabitants to sell as slaves.

These excursions took the pirates as far as the outskirts of Pyongyang on the River Taedong in northwestern Korea. Wokou depredations were so destabilizing that in 1392, they prompted the demise of the Goryeo Dynasty of Korea. The Goryeo were replaced by the Joseon Dynasty, founded by Yi Seonggye (1335–1408), who took the title of King Taejo. Even before he came to power, Taejo, who had been instrumental in improving the Korean military, promoted a very tough line against pirates. In 1380, the extensive wokou fleet that appeared at the mouth of the River Geum in southern Korea was shattered by Korean cannon fire. In 1389, a Korean raid on Tsushima, one of the major wokou bases, was so devastating that some 300 pirate ships were destroyed and several houses onshore set on fire. For good measure, the attackers broke into the jails on Tsushima and released around 100 Korean prisoners.

THE OEI INVASION

Tsushima came under attack again on June 19, 1419, when the Koreans declared war on the island and mounted what the Japanese later called the Oei Invasion. This time, the Koreans played a cunning hand. A large wokou fleet had been gathering on Tsushima, but the Koreans waited until the ships had left harbor on another of their raiding expeditions. Then, with the wokou out of the way, the Koreans set about destroying Tsushima's pirate bases. The Korean fleet of 227 vessels entered the bay between the two islands of Tsushima and, on the next day, put 17,285 soldiers ashore. These proceeded to plunder homes and buildings, destroy crops, kill islanders, and generally create mayhem. The Koreans burned all but 20 of the 129 ships they found at anchor and in a series of skirmishes killed 200 more islanders and captured some 600 prisoners.

But next, the Koreans were pulled up short. Encountering an army, they mistakenly identified it as pirates. They soon discovered their error when the "pirates"—in reality, highly trained samurai—caught them in an ambush. Two hundred Koreans were killed in what the locals termed the Battle of Nukadake. Sadamori (1385–1452), a member of the So clan that ruled Tsushima, called for a ceasefire and subtly reminded the Koreans that at this time of year, the typhoon season was about to begin.

Psychologically this was a stroke of genius, for the devastation wrought on Kublai Khan's fleets by the typhoons of 1274 and particularly 1281 was still fresh

Psychologically this was a stroke of genius, for the devastation wrought on Khan's fleets by the typhoons of 1274 and particularly 1281 was still fresh in Korean minds.

in Korean minds. In any case, Sadamori was speaking no more than the truth: the kamikaze was still a dangerous reality in the waters surrounding Japan. The invaders got the message and withdrew from Tsushima. Japanese prisoners were released after an emissary from the So clan offered the Joseon government tributes of copper and sulfur. By 1443, after more than 20 years of good relations, the head of the So clan was permitted to organize some 50 voyages to Korea each year and his family became "gatekeepers," regulating the flow of trade. Quite unexpectedly, therefore, the Korean raid on Tsushima, intended as a punitive expedition, turned out to have a happy ending. But as Sadamori and the So clan fully realized, everything depended on their ability to put a stop to wokou activity. They could not afford to fail and within ten years of the raid, investigators from Korea were able to report:

> If the pirates of the east and west were to join together, there would be no stopping them.... Tsushima is the place where all the pirates gather.... So Sadamori ordered his people not to let pirates from the west take (on) any water.

Portuguese navigators first reached Japan in 1542 after rounding the southern tip of Africa and sailing across the Indian and Pacific oceans. This picture, painted in typical Japanese style, shows the Portuguese ships.

But stopping the wokou was not quite so simple. Tsushima might be closed to pirates, but there was still a lot of other space in which they could operate. This time, it was China itself that came under attack. Chinese territory had been raided in 1308 and 1311, but these were minor excursions. Serious business began in 1358, when the wokou directed a three-pronged assault at the Shandong peninsula, Jiangsu, and the coastal regions south of the River Yangtze delta. At this early stage, China was easy meat for the wokou. The Yuan Dynasty founded by the mighty Kublai Khan had declined to such an extent that it was unable to put up serious resistance. In fact, the Yuan were only 10 years away from being overthrown by a new dynasty, the Ming. The Ming proved far more durable, and took up the pirate challenge as soon as they came to power in 1368.

In 1358, the wokou pirates were mounting damaging attacks on the Chinese coast, but the first emperor of the Ming dynasty in China, Zhu Huanzang, shown here, was determined to get rid of them.

HUANZANG'S THREAT

The following year, an envoy from the first Ming Emperor Zhu Huanzang (1328–1398) arrived in Japan with an uncompromising message. A clear threat was spelled out, promising a Chinese invasion if the situation were not rectified.

"Japanese pirates repeatedly plunder areas along the coast," it read, "separating men from their wives and children and destroying property and lives." Zhu went on to say that either the Japanese must send tribute to the emperor and become a vassal of China—in which case, presumably, Zhu would send his own forces to deal with the problem—or the Japanese would handle the wokou themselves and use military force to make sure the pirates stayed at home. However, Zhu continued, "if there are those who nonetheless continue to engage in piracy, I will be compelled to order naval officers to set sail for Japan."

The choice offered by Emperor Zhu was not all it seemed. In fact, according to Zhu, there was no choice to be made because, he contended, Japan had already been a vassal state of China for nearly 2000 years, ever since the Japanese came under the aegis of the Han Dynasty (202BC–220CE). It mattered little whether or not the Japanese concurred with this idea. In 1369, Japan was once again convulsed by civil war, this time between rival emperors of the "Northern" and "Southern" courts. However, without any sanction to do so, Prince Kanenaga (1329–83), who commanded forces in the west on behalf of the Southern Court, took it upon himself to send a reply to the Emperor Zhu. The Prince's initial instinct, in 1371, was to execute the Chinese envoys, but instead he sent his own ambassadors to China to offer the tribute demanded by Zhu.

The Emperor was fooled for a time—until, that is, he discovered that the Prince had no authority to offer tribute or, indeed, to make any proposal on behalf of the Japanese state: the civil war ensured that no single individual, and certainly not Kanenaga, had the power to make such decisions. The situation was further complicated when Chinese rebels opposed to the Ming Dynasty requested that a contingent of samurai cross over to China to implement what turned out to be an attempt to assassinate Emperor Zhu. The plot was discovered and the rebels were executed, but the episode so soured Sino–Japanese trade relations that any chance of accord vanished.

The plot was discovered and the rebels were executed, but the episode so soured Sino–Japanese trade relations that any chance of accord vanished.

FEUDAL PIRATES

With the friendlier relations that followed, trade with China and also with Korea became feasible once again. There was some backsliding by the Japanese *daimyos* (feudal lords), who indulged in minor piracy and smuggling in the independent enclaves that the Koreans allowed them at Busan and Jinhae on the southeast coast and Yompo on the east coast. Though small in scale, these activities greatly irked the Koreans and could have been calmed down if the Shogunate intervened to bring their errant feudal lords to order. Unfortunately, the Shoguns were not always able to do this. During the Age of the Warring States, which lasted from 1467 to 1615, their power in Japan waned, waxed, and then waned again under the impetus of various rivalries and civil wars that limited the ability of shoguns to gain power and hold on to it.

Oda Nobunaga (1534–1582) was probably the most influential daimyo in sixteenth-century Japan. One of his greatest achievements was to modernize the samurai fighting forces by developing firearms, ironclad ships, and castle fortifications.

By this time, the composition of the wokou pirate bands had altered. Only around one-third were actually Japanese: the rest were Chinese.

With that, legal trade with China abruptly ceased, and the wokou pirates were in business again. But they would have only 30 years to make the most of it. Another twist in the tale occurred in 1392, when the Shogun Ashikaga Yoshimitsu (1358–1408) managed to broker peace between the Northern and Southern courts of Japan. This restored the somewhat tattered authority of the Shogunate and Japan's trading relations with China came too. Shogun Yoshimitsu, a prudent man, renewed the payment of tribute to the Chinese emperor, who, in return, gave him the title "King of Japan."

The rivalries and civil wars overturned the balance of power in Japan and the ensuing anarchy permitted pirates to return to their old habits. In 1506 and 1509, for example, there were three pirate raids on the Korean island of Gadeok, near present-day Pusan on the southeast coast, and buildings in nearby Jinhae were set on fire in a series of arson attacks. The on-again, off-again Sino–Japanese relationship was once more in a state of flux after 1548, when an argument over Japanese tribute led the Ming Emperor Zhu Houzong (1507–66) to sever all contact with Japan. This, of course, once more ended legitimate trade with China, and the wokou quickly took advantage. Between 1551 and 1560, they escalated the number of their raids on China to 467, some 95 percent above the count for the previous 10 years.

By this time, the composition of the wokou pirate bands had altered. Only around one-third were actually Japanese: the rest were Chinese. One reason for this change lay in the reclusive nature of later Ming emperors. They frequently banned trade with neighboring countries and made it plain that voyages by Chinese sailors and navigators were not to their liking. In this way, the Ming

Dynasty kept foreigners out and ensured Chinese adventurers were kept in. A line of watchtowers, beacons, and fortresses was built to protect the Chinese coastline from Korea to Vietnam. These defenses were regarded as the "Great Wall of the Sea," the southern equivalent to the Great Wall of China in the north.

BAND OF BROTHERS

In 1548, Liampoo island on the Chinese east coast had been a base extensively used by Portuguese traders. It was destroyed, however, by Zhu Wan (1494–1550), the governor of Zhejiang province, who sought to curtail its position as a haven for pirates. Liampoo might be gone, but the notorious Chinese Xu brothers, who had governed it, now served as role models for other pirates who were keen to acquire their share—and maybe more than their share—of the loot that piracy

Toyotomi Hideyoshi, Regent of Japan, was instrumental in suppressing the wokou pirates in the 1570s. He was also a brilliant administrator and businessman, and increased the output of the Kunimoto firearms factory.

could bring them. Transferring to the wokou pirates gave them all the opportunity they needed.

In addition, big pirate boss types were interested in taking over the wokou organization. This they did by first of all creating new bases in Japan, including castles and other fortifications built on islands or hilltops with uninterrupted views of the surrounding area. Some of them enabled the wokou bosses to survey the channels in and around the Inland Sea, which were used by the most lucrative traffic. This virtually guaranteed the wokou substantial profits.

The wokou bosses also recruited samurai as smugglers on a grand scale and hired fresh pirate recruits among the Japanese living in western Honshu, Kyushu, and Shikoko. The Portuguese were in the mix, even including one of their own ambassadors, who was caught pirating in 1523. This revelation lost the Portuguese their trading concessions in Guangdong, which had a long and potentially lucrative coast on the South China Sea, and made the Portuguese switch to piracy inevitable.

Once a haunt of pirates, Macau island, off the southern coast of China, was ceded to Portugal in 1557 and remained under Portuguese control until it was handed back to China in 1999.

This was how an international "band of brothers" became the new wokou pirates and the new scourge of the Chinese coast, which they attacked and sacked with a frequency that made the "Great Wall of the Sea" seem a feeble defense indeed. In 1539, a Chinese merchant called Wang Zhi, later known as the King of the Wokou, made himself head of a trading consortium that protected its operations by means of a large, well-armed fleet. Wang had expected the imperial ban on overseas trade to be lifted, but in 1551, the Ming Emperor Zhou Houzong (1521–1566) tightened it up instead. Wang's reaction was to turn to piracy. He ordered extensive attacks on official buildings, county and district treasuries, and granaries. The surrounding countryside was, of course, affected and along the Zhejiang coast, several towns and villages set up high palisades for security.

These defenses, however, were not equal to the task of keeping out Wang Zhi or the wokou. In 1552, Wang Zhi sent hundreds of pirates to assault places sited all along the coast of Zheijiang; and in 1553, several hundred ships repeated the exercise. Garrisons that were supposed to be on guard to frustrate the attacks were taken prisoner for as long as the plundering lasted. Another year went by and the wokou were building their own fortifications along the Zhejiang coast, where large numbers of pirates came together to prepare for long-distance assaults into Chinese territory. These campaigns took them to within reach of great cities as far distant as the delta of the River Yantze. Hangzou, Suzhou, and Nanjing were other major conurbations listed for attack. Ultimately, the wokou forts and bases along the Zheijiang coast were manned by up to 20,000 pirates.

The Chinese were fortunate to have two superlative commanders to fight back against the wokou: Qi Jiguang (1528–88) and Yu Dayou (1503–79), both highly experienced leaders. Natives of the coastal areas under attack, both were skilled in the art of sea warfare. In 1553, forces led by Yu Dayou stormed the island of Putuoshan off the coast of Zheijang, where the wokou had a major camp, and sent the pirates packing. Two years later, Dayou caught a wokou force north of Jiaxing, which was also in Zhejiang, and killed around 2000 of them. Qi Jiguang lead the 4000-strong force, known as the Qi Family Army, consisting mainly of miners and farmers. In 1555, to defend Taizhou, a coastal city of Zheijang, the Army fought a series of engagements against Wang Zhi and the wokou forces.

The work of Qi Jiguang and Yu Dayou was vital to turn back the tide of piracy of Wang Zhi and the international wokou forces, but unlike them, the real nemesis of the pirates was not Chinese. He was Toyotomi Hideyoshi (1536–98), a Japanese *daimyo* (feudal lord) who became *kampaku* (regent) of Japan in 1585. Hideyoshi started life as a lowly samurai, but enjoyed an extraordinary rise to power and influence in Japan as the foremost general to the powerful daimyo Oda Nobunaga (1534–82). Hideyoshi was later dubbed "the Napoleon of Japan" for his exploits in bringing down the kaizuku pirates causing havoc inside Japan using large-scale, brilliantly executed invasions of Shikoku (1585) and Kyushu (1587). These operations featured large numbers of samurai warriors shipped into the battle zones for the purpose, and finally put an end to 30 years of pirating by the Murakami family of Hiroshima and saw to the destruction of their bases.

JAPANESE SOCIETY INSTIGATES REFORMS

Three years later, Hideyoshi initiated fundamental reforms throughout Japanese society, several of which counted as brakes on pirates and piracy. First, weapons

Hideyoshi started life as a lowly samurai, but enjoyed an extraordinary rise to power and influence in Japan as the foremost general to the powerful daimyo Oda Nobunaga.

were to be confined to the *daimyos* and the samurai warrior class. This effectively made possessing them illegal for everyone else, including pirates. Later, in 1591, the samurai were formally separated from the rest of Japanese society, thus emphasizing their monopoly of military activities. A further edict required Japanese seamen and navigators to take an oath not to indulge in piracy. If by any chance daimyos, a class that had themselves flirted with piracy in the past, allowed pirates to ply their trade, they would be deprived of the lands they held in fief. Land tenure provided the basis for their position as feudal warlords, so this edict meant that offending daimyos would be ruined. As it was, the freedoms they had once enjoyed without restraint—to carry arms, raid, plunder, destroy, and terrorize populations—had been curtailed.

In any event, these edicts never needed to be carried out because, despite alarming appearances, the strength of the wokou had been declining for some time. As far back as 1566–57, the Portuguese and the Ming Emperor Zhu Zaihu (died 1573) had been implementing joint action against the wokou. Although they were odd bedfellows, this partnership made sense as far as the Chinese were concerned. Portuguese ships were better armed and more formidable than local vessels and their very presence in harbor or out at sea was daunting even for the wokou pirates. It seems that in return for their co-operation, the Portuguese were allowed to settle in Macau, an enclave on the southeast coast of China, which they retained for more than four centuries until 1999. Possibly as a result of this Sino–Portuguese accord, the Chinese came to their senses at last in 1567 and lifted the ban on overseas trade. Many wokou deserted the exciting but risky pirate life to return to legal trading. This made good sense because legal trade became more profitable than piracy now that the Portuguese were able to sell goods from India and Indonesia at better prices than the wokou could afford.

The shogunate's misgivings were based largely on the fact that the converts, who numbered 300,000, now owed their loyalty to the pope in Rome.

THE END OF THE WOKOU PIRATES

However, the end of the wokou pirates came about not through market forces, military onslaughts, or even the exploits of pirate hunters like Yu Dayou, Qi Jiguang, or the great Tomotori Hideyoshi, but something entirely unconnected with either pirates or piracy. The catalyst for the demise of the wokou was the increasing mistrust held by the Tokugawa shogunate (who came to power in Japan in 1603) against Roman Catholic missionaries and their converts. The

WOKOU PIRACY FURTHER AFIELD

Before Wokou piracy was extinguished forever, the pirates enjoyed a long, but final, fling in places far distant from their previous haunts in China and Korea. After Toyotomi Hideyoshi died in 1598, the pirates ravaged targets in South East Asia, including the Spice Islands of Indonesia, and Siam (Thailand), Vietnam, and Cambodia in the Indochinese peninsula. Wokou depredations also reached across the Pacific Ocean to the Philippine Islands, which became a Spanish possession after 1565. These raids so alarmed the authorities that in 1605, after many years' experience of the wokou threat, the Spanish governor of the Philippines began to fear that a full-scale pirate invasion was imminent.

shogunate's misgivings were based largely on the fact that the converts, who numbered 300,000, now owed their loyalty to the pope in Rome. The Tokugawa regarded the pope as a foreign, and therefore subversive, ruler who needed to be expunged from Japanese life. Some selective persecution of Christians had taken place before the advent of the Tokugawa, notably in 1597, when Hideyoshi banished missionaries from Japan and executed several foreign priests, but the Tokugawa shoguns had no patience with half measures. In 1633, Iemitsu (1604–51), the third Tokugawa shogun, issued the first of three "Seclusion edicts," which banned the practice of the Christian religion in Japan. The second, issued in 1635, hit directly at traders and pirates alike: travel outside Japan was forbidden except for a small number of license-holders. Anyone who dared return home after an illicit voyage would be executed, a punishment designed not only to get rid of them but also to prevent them spreading their knowledge of foreign parts to anyone else. The third edict of 1639 finally closed the door by banning the Portuguese (who had come to Japan as both pirates and missionaries) from entering any Japanese port. In July 1640, a Portuguese captain and crew sailed into Nagasaki harbor, hoping to persuade Shogun Iemitsu to change his mind. However, for this piece of temerity, 57 crewmen were decapitated. Hapless sailors shipwrecked on the shores of Japan were treated in the same way, so desperate were the shoguns to block any information about the outside world from penetrating the shut-away enclave they had made of Japan.

The Japanese slumbered on in their feudal isolation for more than two centuries until 1853, when the United States forced them to open up their ports to international trade and shipping and so join the modern world. But for all that time, the Seclusion Edicts severed the wokou, the kaizuku, and other pirates from everything that had once made them rich, successful, and profoundly feared. Their sources of plunder were now placed beyond their reach. So were the victims, who had once offered "protection money," and the foreign rulers who, for their own benefit, had cynically exploited the pirates' ability to terrorize entire coasts along with their towns, villages and populations. Now, without the oxygen of opportunity, the wokou were history.

Ieyasu (1543–1616) became the first Tokugawa Shogun of Japan in 1603. The Tokugawa shogunate, which was founded by Ieyasu, ruled Japan until the country began to modernize in 1868.

chapter 4

PIRATE DEMOCRACY

A pirate ship may seem a curious place to discover democratic values in practice when democracies were hard to find elsewhere in the seventeenth or eighteenth centuries. Yet the pirate codes of the time, such as those authored by Bartholomew Roberts (1682–1722) in 1720 and Captain John Phillips (died 1724) in 1724, promoted egalitarian ideas. Among them were equal voting rights for the whole crew on important decisions, equal access to fresh provisions, and the same punishments for any miscreant on board, even the captain and the Quartermaster. The Quartermaster, who was in charge of discipline onboard and thus the real master of a pirate ship, was elected by the pirate crew—as was, sometimes, the captain.

This equality might not seem so strange when viewed against the realities of life three and four centuries ago. In an age when poverty, starvation, and untreatable disease stalked the everyday existence of millions, life could be merciless. Such conditions brutalized populations, as did the draconian punishments used to keep them in order. In Britain, by the end of the eighteenth century, the so-called Bloody Code included more than 200 felonies punishable by death, and such crimes as stealing animals, concealing bankruptcy, or maliciously maiming cattle were among them.

A galleon (right) fires a broadside at a pirate vessel as its heavily armed crew wait for the moment when their ship can move alongside, enabling them to come aboard.

This was a cruel world, and pirates, who frequently came from the most desperate sections of society, often regarded piracy as a way out of its toils. Piracy, of course, imposed its own rules, which could be just as harsh when it came to penalties for misdemeanors. Theft, for example, was punished by one of two methods: the guilty man was either shot or marooned, which meant being abandoned on a small island and left there with some food, water, and a loaded gun. Marooning was effectively a death sentence; many marooned pirates used the loaded gun to commit suicide.

The codes of piracy, however, provided a bonus not available in the outside world, such as access to material advantage that was not confined to the already

Bartholomew Roberts became a pirate after he was captured by a pirate ship and "converted" to a life of piracy. But like many pirates, his career was short: it lasted only three years.

DIVIDE AND CONQUER

Some pirates were men with valuable seafaring skills, such as navigators or carpenters. Others were men who had been captured in raids and forced to join the crew and sign Articles of Agreement. In time, these captives-turned-pirates could grow accustomed to, or even appreciate, the life that was forced on them, but they might also fiercely resent their fate and seek to escape it at the first opportunity. In these circumstances, a pirate captain could not entirely trust his crew. Never certain of their true temper, he was on his own, secure in his position only by his force of personality, the success of the raids he led and the wealth they yielded, and his code, which effectively set every member of his crew watching all the others to see that no one seized undue advantage and cheated anyone else.

rich, influential, and fortunate, but was there in equal measure for anyone onboard ship, however lowly. The codes, generally known as Articles of Agreement, could be made for a specific length of time, for a pirating season or even for just one voyage. But they were not entirely civilized arrangements. First of all, codes were sealed by oaths that exploited the superstitious nature innate in seafarers. Some of these oaths were sworn on the Bible—taken to mean in the presence of God. Others were taken on crossed pistols, axes, human skulls, or while sitting astride a cannon. Such rituals were guaranteed frighteners, because violence and death were involved in all of them. Once signed by each crew member, the codes were displayed in a place such as the main cabin of a ship, where everyone could see them and so be reminded of their provisions.

If the codes represented discipline for pirates, they also served as protection, by limiting, usually on pain of death, the type and severity of the crimes that could be committed against them. This applied to the captain more than anyone else. Most captains of pirate ships were freelance raiders, hiring their own crews and, as it were, running their own business. In this context, there was no room for the official rules that applied to the captains of naval vessels or even merchantmen, where rank had its privileges and most crewmen knew their place.

Pirate captains, by contrast, had to deal with a volatile crew who were accustomed to destroy, steal, and kill. They promised no assurance of loyalty or obedience and there was certainly no guarantee of civilized conduct on board ship. It was said that pirates

> were almost always mad or drunk, their behavior produced infinite disorders, every man being, in his own imagination, a captain, a prince or king...they eat in a very disorderly manner, more like a kennel of hounds than like men, snatching and catching the victuals from one another.

Marooning was effectively a death sentence; many marooned pirates used the loaded gun to commit suicide.

BLACK BART

Bartholomew Roberts, or Black Bart as he was referred to after his death, was a colorful character with a habit of dressing for battle in his most brilliant and expensive finery. In 1724, Charles Johnson wrote a description of him in

This oil painting shows a fictional scene: two pirates fighting over the command of their ship. In real life, the pirate code allowed a crew to elect their captain—or, if necessary, depose him.

A General History of the Robberies and Murders of the Most Notorious Pirates. Johnson wrote:

Roberts himself made a gallant figure. At the time of an engagement, [he would be] dressed in a rich crimson damask waistcoat and breeches, a red feather in his hat, a gold chain around his neck with a diamond cross hanging to it, a sword in his hand and two pairs of pistols slung over his shoulders.

This habit of showing himself off in all his finery ultimately contributed to his death, but by then Bartholomew Roberts was already the most successful pirate chief of the so-called Golden Age of Piracy. Roberts was highly skilled in the art of leading his crews in lucrative raids and retaining their loyalty while he filled their pockets. His career lasted only three years from 1719–22, but in that brief time, he is reckoned to have captured and plundered around 470 vessels.

Born in Pembrokeshire, Wales, in 1682, Bartholomew Roberts first went to sea at the age of 13 in 1695. In 1719, Roberts was working as third mate on the slave ship *Princess of London* while it was at anchor at Anonmabu off the coast of present-day Ghana. The *Princess* was probably waiting to embark its human cargo when two pirate ships attacked the vessel. Roberts was among those taken prisoner. He soon displayed the sort of navigational skills that made him useful to the pirate captain, Howell Davis (died 1719), another Welshman, who demanded that Roberts join his crew. Roberts, it seems, was reluctant at first, but quickly realized the advantages. He said later,

In an honest service there is thin commons, low wages and hard labor.... In this (there is) plenty and satiety, pleasure and ease, liberty and power.... No, a merry life and a short one shall be my motto.

But the dangers of the "merry life and a short one" soon made themselves evident. Not long after Roberts joined his crew, Captain Davis was killed during an attempted raid on the Portuguese-ruled island of Principe off the coast of West Africa. Six weeks later, the crew elected Roberts to replace Captain Davis, whose death he set out to avenge. Roberts and his crew stormed the island of Principe by night, killed most of the male population and stole every valuable item they could lay their hands on. After that, Roberts captured a Dutch vessel and then an English ship named *Experiment*. While at Anaboe off the coast of present-day Ghana, where the pirates took on water and provisions, the crew voted for their next destination. The choice was the West Indies or Brazil. The crew decided on the latter. At first, it did not seem a good choice. The *Royal Rover* hung around the Brazilian coast for nine weeks without sighting any ships. The crew was about to give up and sail for the West Indies when a fleet of 42 Portuguese vessels appeared in Todos os Santos Bay, along the coast of Bahia province.

The fleet was awaiting the arrival of two powerful 70-gun men-o'-war, which were to escort them across the Atlantic Ocean to Portugal. Bartholomew Roberts and the *Royal Rover* got there first. The pirates captured the richest of the Portuguese merchantmen, a 40-gun vessel crewed by 170 men, and took its cargo of 40,000 gold moidors and a mass of jewelry, which included a cross set with diamonds specially designed for the Portuguese king, Joao V (1706–50).

Heavy drinking was virtually endemic among pirate crews and their captains. An exception was Bartholomew Roberts, who was known as a "sober man." He tried, but failed, to discourage drinking among his men.

WHILE CAPTAIN WAS ABSENT

Roberts' first few weeks in charge of a pirate vessel had been pleasantly lucrative, but he was about to experience another peril of his new and infamous trade—the faithlessness and greed of one of his lieutenants, Walter Kennedy (died 1721). Roberts' mistake was to leave Kennedy in charge of the the *Royal Rover*, the majority of its crew and its cargo of booty. Meanwhile, Roberts took 40 of his crewmen, captured a sloop off the coast of Surinam in South America and chased after a supposedly well-stocked brigantine. Kennedy took advantage of Roberts' absence by proclaiming himself captain and sailing back across the Atlantic toward his native Ireland. His navigation was so poor—unlike Roberts'—that he landed instead on the northwestern coast of Scotland. He was later captured and hanged as a pirate at Execution Dock in London.

Bartholomew Roberts, left with only his sloop and a much reduced crew, decided to bring some kind of order into the chaotic pirate world,

where, as William Kennedy had shown, self-interest too often prevailed over other considerations. Thus he established a code that set out, for the benefit of all, the terms of future pirating. This was not a new idea, nor was Roberts the first to control his crew in this way, but in the context of pirate society, a code was a reminder that even among thieves there should be some honor.

Roberts began by emphasizing the code's democratic fair-share credentials, but also included the first of several dire warnings about the severe punishment that awaited cheats and fraudsters. The two provisions stated,

> Every man shall have an equal vote in the affairs of the moment. He shall have an equal title to the fresh provisions or strong liquors at any time seized and shall use them at pleasure unless scarcity may make it necessary for the common good that a retrenchment may be voted.
>
> Every man shall be called fairly in turn by the list on board of prizes, because over and above their proper share, they are allowed a shift of clothes.

Next, though, came the first of the stern warnings, which included savage disfigurement:

> But if they defraud the company to the value of even one dollar in plate, jewels or money, they shall be marooned. If any man rob another, he shall have his nose and ears slit, and be put ashore where he shall be sure to encounter hardships.

Gaming at cards or dicing for money was banned, a wise precaution when pirates might be tempted to fritter away their loot and then replace their losses by theft. Sore losers could also turn violent. An attempt to curtail drinking was also made by the order that

> lights and candles should be put out at eight at night, and if any of the crew desire to drink after that hour, they shall sit upon the open deck without lights.

Bartholomew Roberts himself was known as a "sober man" and doubtless hoped that if his code took the pleasure out of drinking by

Pirate treasure could come in many forms. There were gold and silver plates, cups and coins, jewels and jewelry, splendidly decorated statues, rare textiles like silk or brocades, and occasional quantities of food.

confining his men to the dark, open deck "after hours," this might prompt them to give it up altogether. It was a well-meaning attempt, but drinking was a habit far too strongly entrenched in eighteenth-century life and Roberts never managed to make his crew teetotal.

The fifth provision in Roberts' code was a call to duty, requiring each man to "keep his piece, cutlass and pistols at all times clean and ready for action." This command was probably superfluous. Pirates in Roberts' time were inordinately proud of their weapons, and even vied with each other to see who could have the most elaborate and beautifully decorated pistols. Pirates were also willing to spend considerable sums on their weapons, and when auctions were held onboard ship, it was not unusual for them to bid $59 (£30) or $79 (£40) if it meant acquiring a superlative piece. The pirates even went so far as to sling their pistols over their shoulders on vibrantly colorful ribbons.

In the sixth of Roberts' provisions, he returned to his somewhat puritanical desire to excise sin from the lives of his crew. "No boy or woman to be allowed," the code insisted. "If any shall be found seducing any of the latter sex and carrying her to sea in disguise, he shall suffer death." Even so, there was a loophole: if a woman were found aboard a pirate ship, it seems that a sentinel was at once appointed to guard her. But there was no guard over the sentinel who, more often than not, himself "secured the lady's virtue" as the coy expression went, and stopped anyone else from having her.

After this, came the seventh provision of Bartholomew Roberts' code, its meaning unambiguous: "he that shall desert the ship or his quarters in time of

Pirate codes frequently banned or warned against gambling among pirate crews. Gambling generated the sort of excitement that could make gamblers aggressive and fight each other or tempt them to steal to retrieve losses.

THE PIRATE CODE

Most pirate codes forbade women to be brought on board ship. Not only were they considered unlucky, but pirates tended to fight over them, or treat them brutally, often resulting in rape and death.

battle shall be punished by death or marooning." The eighth provision was similarly harsh,

> None shall strike another on board the ship, but every man's quarrel shall be ended on shore by sword or pistol.... At the word of command from the Quartermaster, each man being previously placed back to back shall turn and fire immediately. If any man do not, the Quartermaster shall knock the piece out of his hand. If both (contestants) miss their aim, they shall take to their cutlasses and he that draweth first blood shall be declared the victor.

The ninth provision dealt with the compensation a man could expect should he be so badly injured that he was unfit to pursue piracy as a profession:

> Every man who shall become a cripple or lose a limb in the service, shall have 800 pieces of eight from the common stock and for lesser hurts proportionately.

Despite the democratic character of much of the Roberts code, booty was shared according to the crew's hierarchy. The tenth provision stated:

> The captain and the Quartermaster shall each receive two shares of a prize, the master gunner and boatswain, one and one half shares, all other officers one and one quarter and private gentlemen of fortune—the rest of the crew— one share each.

The final, eleventh provision stipulated that the ship's musicians were to "have by right rest on the Sabbath day only. On all other days, by favor only."

Once these terms had been agreed and the pirate crew signed up to them, Bartholomew Roberts resumed his hunt for the riches to be had along the eastern seaboards of the Americas. Roberts' sloop, appropriately renamed *Fortune*, headed north and in June 1720 appeared off the coast of Newfoundland. With its indented coastline and large number of small islands, Newfoundland offered him ideal conditions. As pirates before him had done since ancient times, Roberts hid out of sight until a ship came by that was likely to prove a prize catch, then swooped out to seize his prey. On June 21, the *Fortune* created widespread panic when she penetrated the large harbor at Trepassey, close by the Grand Banks of Newfoundland, flying the black flags that told crews already at anchor that they could expect no quarter. Captains and crews at once abandoned ship and fled. About a week later, the *Fortune* sailed out of Trepassey, headed for the Caribbean. But before she left, all ships in the harbor were set alight.

Roberts spent another nine months among the Caribbean islands, where he captured more than 50 ships and, it seems, nearly brought trade in the West Indies to a halt. By this time, he commanded three vessels—the *Royal Fortune* (the *Fortune* renamed) and two captured French warships, which he named *Ranger* and *Little Ranger*. Around the end of January 1722, the three ships left the Caribbean, heading for the coast of West Africa. They arrived at Cape Lopez in present-day Gabon, where, on February 10, they were discovered careening by the Royal Navy warship HMS *Swallow*. With its 50 guns, the *Swallow* was more powerful than Roberts' best-armed ship, the 16-gun *Ranger*, and this superiority soon told in the ensuing battle. Roberts planned to sail past the *Swallow* in *Royal Fortune*, allowing the *Swallow* only enough time to loose one broadside. If the pirate ship survived, she could sail out of danger. But the helmsman on the *Royal Fortune* failed to follow the right course. The *Swallow* managed to fire off a second broadside and Roberts was killed (*see* box, below).

JOHN PHILLIPS

John Phillips became a pirate in the same way as Bartholomew Roberts. In the summer of 1723, Phillips, as a shipwright, joined a vessel that was about to sail to Newfoundland. On the way, the ship was captured by a pirate brigantine, the 18-gun *Good Fortune*, commanded by Thomas Anstis (died 1723), who had previously served with Howell Davis and Bartholomew Roberts. As a carpenter

Roberts spent another nine months among the Caribbean islands, where he captured more than 50 ships and, it seems, nearly brought trade in the West Indies to a halt.

THE DEATH OF BARTHOLOMEW ROBERTS

During the battle with the Royal Navy ship HMS *Swallow*, Bartholomew Roberts stood on deck in all his finery, as was his habit, and made a highly conspicuous target. He received a blast of grapeshot in the throat and died instantly. It was well known that Roberts had always wanted to be buried at sea and his crew carried out his wishes. They wrapped his body in the ship's sail, weighed it down, and threw it overboard. It was never recovered. Two pirates were also killed in the battle, which went on for another two hours until the *Royal Fortune*'s mainmast came crashing down and the surviving pirates asked for quarter. A total of 272 pirates were captured and, of these, 54 were later hanged in London.

RISKING THE DEATH PENALTY

One of John Phillips' earliest experiences as a pirate almost ended his career and his life. While on its way from the Caribbean to the coast of West Africa, *Good Fortune* captured a ship from County Cork in Ireland. Among the passengers was a young woman, who was brutally attacked by Captain Anstis and some of his men. One of the male passengers, an army colonel, tried to defend her but was soon kicked out of the way while Anstis and his pirates continued molesting the woman. At last, when they had finished with her, they killed her and threw her body overboard.

by trade, Phillips was a valuable addition to the pirate crew. He was, of course, in no position to refuse Captain Anstis' "invitation" and duly joined up.

Whether or not the *Good Fortune*'s crew had signed up to a pirate code is unknown, but all the same, it was a generally accepted rule onboard ship that attacks on women incurred the death penalty (*see* box above). Certainly, the pirates of the *Good Fortune* became thoroughly scared by what had happened and began to plan how to exonerate themselves. Some chose to ask the King of England, George I, for a pardon. Others decided to ignore the whole thing and keep on pirating. Eventually, it was agreed that once they had reached the Caribbean island of Tobago, a petition should be sent to England onboard a merchant ship. Also onboard were several of the crew who, unlike some others, were sure they would be pardoned. One of them was John Phillips. The rest of the crew (six or eight men) stayed behind on the island of Tobago, but this proved to be no shelter for them. They were later arrested and taken to Antigua, some 500 miles (800km) to the north, where all but one of them were hanged.

PHILLIPS SETS SAIL IN *REVENGE*

However, while he was in England, Phillips was warned by some of his friends that King George had no interest in the pirates' petition for a pardon and that some of those who had returned with him were already in prison. Realizing that he could easily be next, Phillips joined a vessel bound for Newfoundland. Once he got there, Phillips persuaded four other pirates to join him and seized an American schooner from Boston at anchor in the harbor of St Pierre on the south coast of Newfoundland. On the night of August 29, 1723, the pirates sailed the schooner out of the harbor. They renamed the vessel *Revenge* and John Phillips was elected captain.

Subsequently, the pirates captured a number of fishing vessels whose crews were obliged to join them. Before long, the *Revenge* had a sizeable crew of its own. Among them was an experienced pirate, John Rose Archer (died 1724), who had once served under the famous pirate known as Blackbeard, Edward Teach. Archer was elected Quartermaster.

Nevertheless, the new intake caused problems. Although he had been a pirate for only a few weeks, Phillips had seen enough of pirate behavior to be fully aware that he needed a code of some sort if order were to be maintained onboard the *Revenge*. The Articles of Agreement Phillips drew up in 1724 sought mainly to cut off avenues of misbehavior and so included far more stick than carrot. His

> **Among them was an experienced pirate, John Rose Archer, who had once served under the famous pirate known as Blackbeard, Edward Teach. Archer was elected Quartermaster.**

code began with the stricture that "every man shall obey civil command." It went on to set out the shares of booty yielded in successful raids:

> The Captain shall have one full share and a half of all prizes. The Quartermaster, Carpenter, Boatswain and Gunner shall have one share and a quarter.

Although not specifically mentioned, the rest of the crew presumably received what was left on an equal-shares basis.

The next six provisions of John Phillips' articles contained threats of punishment for various misdemeanors. This represented two-thirds of his code, which says something about the brutality and fecklessness Phillips expected from the pirates onboard his ship. For example, in the second provision, marooning was the punishment laid down "if any man shall...run away or keep any secret" from the crew. The third provision was concerned with theft:

> If any man shall steal anything from the crew or game, to the value of a piece of eight, he shall be marooned or shot.

The fourth provision gave Phillips and his crew the right to choose the penalty to be paid by any man who signed the Articles of Agreement of a rival pirate captain. The fifth invoked "Moses' law" for "that man that shall strike

HMS *Swallow* fires broadsides at a pirate ship that is flying a skull and crossbones pirate flag and firing back. The *Swallow* brought an end to Bartholomew Roberts' career in 1722.

The pirates on *Revenge* who signed up to Phillips' Articles of Agreement apparently had no Bible onboard, and made their oaths with one hand resting on an ax.

another whilst these Articles are in force"—in the form of 39 lashes on the bare back. In the sixth provision, the biblical Law of Moses was also laid down for any man who (fired) his weapon or smoked "tobacco in the hold without a cap to his pipe." These were wise precautions designed to prevent fire onboard ship, an ever-present danger on wooden vessels and the most feared of all disasters among seafarers. Carrying "a candle lighted without a lantern" was also forbidden for the same reason.

The seventh provision in John Phillips' code warned crewmen that anyone who failed to keep his weapons clean and

> fit for engagement, shall be cut off from his share (of the booty) and suffer such other punishment as the captain and the (crew) shall think fit.

This was another wise precaution. Weapons made inefficient by neglect could make the difference between success and defeat in battle against another pirate crew or a pirate-hunter.

Phillips' eighth provision echoed Bartholomew Roberts' ninth, by stipulating that "any man (who) shall lose a joint in time of an engagement shall have 400 pieces of eight, if a limb, 800." The ninth and last provision of the Phillips code reflected his alarming experience when Thomas Anstis, now dead, had been in charge: "If at any time, you meet with a prudent woman, that man that offers to meddle with her without her consent, shall suffer...death." The pirates on *Revenge* who signed up to Phillips' Articles of Agreement apparently had no Bible onboard, and made their oaths with one hand resting on an ax.

MURDER, MUTINY, AND MUTILATION

For the next two months, until October 1723, the *Revenge* and her captain and crew scored remarkable success. Their hunting ground extended from the harbors of Newfoundland all the way south to the island of Barbados, a distance of some 3575 miles (5750km). Along the way, they seized a total of 10 vessels. This yielded numerous prisoners, some of whom, like Bartholomew Roberts and John Phillips himself, joined the pirates and accepted the pirate way of life and, of

Pirates were armed with many different sorts of weapons. The best known was the curved cutless (below), but the flintlock pistol (above) was also frequently used. Other weapons included axes, muskets, grenades, and shipboard cannon.

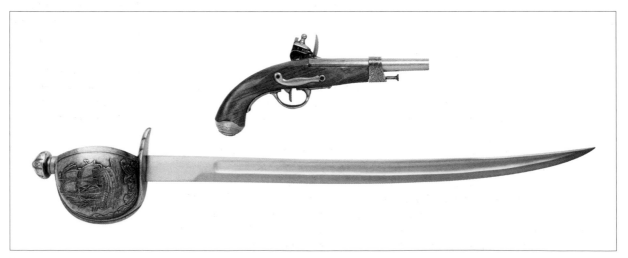

course, its code. Others, though, were kept as prisoners, possibly for sale as slaves. The rest were thrown overboard to drown.

At the beginning of February 1724, the *Revenge* was off Long Island, New York, where the crew captured a scow. Captain Phillips put four of his men onboard with instructions to sail alongside the *Revenge* as they navigated their way southward. But the four pirates had other ideas. They intended to desert. There was a brief but deadly exchange of fire between the scow and the *Revenge*. One of the would-be deserters was killed, two surrendered, and the fourth, William Phillips (no relation to the captain) suffered a serious injury to his left leg. His life was saved—though at what cost in pain is incalculable—when John Phillips amputated his injured leg with his carpenter's saw. He then sealed the bleeding stump by heating an ax until it was red hot and applying it to the wound.

After this, the *Revenge* continued on its way, seizing more ships until John Phillips' total amounted to 37 prizes. As time went on, though, the task was becoming more and more difficult. The *Revenge* was operating in a very crowded area. Phillips was up against strong competition from other pirates who were anxious to seize the rich prizes offered by the North and Central American coastal settlements, and the Caribbean islands. At the end of March 1724, John Phillips seized a ship off Cape Sable, near Halifax, Nova Scotia, and in the struggle for possession was badly wounded when the captain struck him over the head with a handspike. Phillips managed to wound him with a sword thrust, after which his pirates slashed the attacker dead.

Phillips was seriously injured and in no fit state to exercise his command. Although some members of his crew had saved him, others had mutiny in mind. They were disillusioned with Phillips' declining success rate and, it seems, he had also turned too sadistic and bloodthirsty even for his fellow pirates. On April 17, 1724, still in a dazed, disorientated state, he was unable to resist as his men tripped him up on deck and threw him overboard. They watched him drown.

John Phillips' career as a pirate had lasted less than nine months. His murderers went on trial at the Court of Admiralty in Boston in the presence of their erstwhile captain's severed head. (Officers of the court had recovered Phillips' body, cut off the head, pickled it to make sure it remained identifiable and entered it as prosecution evidence.) The pirates on trial were all found guilty and were hanged on Bird Island, in east Boston on June 2 1724. One of them was the veteran pirate John Rose Archer, Phillips' one-time Quartermaster.

These Articles of Agreement were concluded with the privateer Captain William Kidd in 1695. The Agreement set out the rules to be followed during Kidd's ill-fated pirate-hunting voyage to the Indian Ocean.

BARTHOLOMEUS DE PORTUGEES.
Hooft van een partij Franse
en Engelse Rovers,

A page from *The Buccaneers of America*, published in 1678 by Alexander Exquemelin, himself a one-time buccaneer and confidante of Henry Morgan. As a surgeon, Exquemelin took part in the great raid on Cartagena (1697).

The pirate codes of John Phillips and Bartholomew Roberts were only two among many that were agreed and signed and survived. The reason few of these codes were preserved as originally written was that pirates in danger of capture destroyed their copies by burning them or throwing them into the sea. This was an understandable precaution. The code, carrying their signature or mark, identified them as pirates and could be produced at their trials as evidence against them; and those found guilty of piracy were almost routinely sentenced to death.

THE SHARE OF BOOTY

Fortunately, though, other codes survived when they were reproduced in such publications as *The Buccaneers of America.* This was written by Alexander Olivier Exquemelin (*c.*1645–1707), a French former pirate, and first published in 1678. Exquemelin revealed that more than 40 years before Bartholomew Roberts put together his Articles of Agreement in 1720, many of its provisions were already a well-established practice in the pirate community. For example, the share of booty due the captain of a pirate ship was specified, even though some conditions that were in place in the seventeenth century did not necessarily appear in later codes. Among them was the stipulation that booty was shared out only after payments had been made for special services provided. The ship's carpenter was paid between 100 and 150 pieces of eight for his work in repairing and fitting out the vessel. The surgeon received 200 or 250 pieces to pay for his medical supplies, depending on the size of the ship and its crew.

Exquemelin also included awards to compensate injuries, a symptom of the extreme danger to life and limb that active piracy involved. There was, though, a difference between the recompense for the loss of right and left limbs. Prevalent superstitions might explain this apparent paradox. Left-handedness, for example, was often considered a sign of the devil's influence. "Sinister," the Latin word for "left," which the English language borrowed unchanged in translation, had menacing connotations. When applied to the loss of an arm or leg, the right was naturally favored over the left and more was awarded in the way of compensation.

"For the loss of the right arm," Exquemelin wrote "600 pieces and six or eight slaves (would be paid)," but "for a left arm, 500 pieces of eight or five slaves. The loss of a right leg also brought 500 pieces of eight or five slaves in compensation; a left leg, 400 pieces or four slaves.... If a man lost the use of an arm, he would get as much as if it had been cut off." For the loss of an eye or a finger, the compensation was 100 pieces of eight or one slave.

When it came to sharing out the booty after a raid, a pirate captain was naturally accorded more loot than the rest of the crew. This was reckoned at four or five portions for the use of his ship, and two portions for himself. But broadly speaking, the captain was not always as favored as this might suggest. As Exquemelin explained:

> When a ship has been captured, the men decide whether the captain should keep it or not; if the prize is better than their own vessel they take it and set fire to the other.
>
> The captain is allowed no better fare than the meanest on board. If they notice that he has better food, the men bring the dish from their own mess and exchange it for the captain's.

Other rules of the code indicate that precautions had to be taken to counteract dishonesty among men who, after all, spent their lives breaking the law. Exquemelin explained:

> When a ship is robbed nobody must plunder and keep his loot to himself. Everything taken—money, jewels, precious stones and goods—must be shared among them all, without any man enjoying more than his fair share. To prevent deceit, before the booty is distributed, everyone (must) swear oath on the Bible that he has not kept for himself so much as the value of a sixpence, whether in silk, linen, wool, gold, silver, jewels, clothes or shot, from all the capture. And should any man be found to have made a false oath, he would be banished from the (ship) and never more be allowed in the company.

EDWARD LOWE

Another pirate code was preserved in *The Boston Newsletter*, the first regular newspaper in the British American colonies, whose first edition appeared on April 24, 1704. It published a sensational account of the death of Blackbeard (Edward Teach) in 1718 and details of the Articles of Agreement signed by pirates who sailed with Captain Edward Lowe (*c*.1690–1724) and his partner in crime, George Lowther (died 1723).

A brutal pirate, Edward Lowe was notorious for inflicting abominable tortures on his prisoners before killing them. In 1892, *The New York Times* published an article headlined "The 'Great' Edward Lowe: The Most Merciless Pirate Known to Modern Times." This described Lowe as a torturer who would have "done credit to the ingenuity of the Spanish Inquisition in its darkest days." He tied up prisoners' hands with a rope, then set it alight. In a few minutes, the hands were burnt to the bone. Lowe was also reputed to have a burned a French cook alive, having called him "a greasy fellow who would fry well."

Philip Ashton (born *c*.1702) was more fortunate than other prisoners taken by Edward Lowe. Captured in 1722 on the coast of Nova Scotia, he was not tortured, but was put in chains, whipped, and beaten in efforts to force him to join the

Lowe was a torturer…also reputed to have burned a French cook alive, having called him "a greasy fellow who would fry well."

Buccaneers, who specialized in Caribbean piracy, on the island of Hispaniola. This was their base for several years, until they were driven out by the French in 1633 and fled to Tortuga island.

pirate crew. Ashton refused. In 1723, he managed to escape and was eventually rescued. After his return home, he recounted his experiences, including a graphic account of torture sessions that occurred on board Lowe's vessel. Ashton wrote:

> Of all the pyratical crews that were ever heard of, none of the English name came up to this in barbarity. (The crew's) mirth and their anger had much the same effect, for both were usually gratified with the cries and groans of their prisoners; so that they almost as often murdered a man from the excess of good humor as out of passion and resentment, and the unfortunate could never be assured of safety from them, for danger lurked in their very smiles.

It appears that he was a "bad lot" from the start. Born into a life of poverty in Westminster, in London, in around 1690, he soon became a juvenile delinquent. In his *A General History of the Pyrates* published in 1724, Charles Johnson described Lowe as illiterate, quarrelsome, and running "wild in the streets of his native parish." Cheating and stealing came naturally to him and while still young, Lowe was working as a gambler and a pickpocket. Mere thievery, however, was not lucrative enough for him and he turned instead to burglary.

In around 1710, Edward Lowe left England for America. Once there, he worked as a rigger and in 1714, he married. The marriage was doomed to tragedy. Lowe's first child, a son, died in infancy and his wife, Eliza, died giving birth to a daughter in 1719. Lowe was profoundly affected, and later on, as a pirate chief, he was always reluctant to hire married men for his crews. But in response to the loss of his wife and son, he also reverted to violent type. In 1722, Lowe was in Honduras in Central America, as the leader of a 12-man gang, supervising the loading on board ship of a consignment of logs for sale in Boston. One day, Lowe quarreled with the ship's captain, who refused to let him eat when he was hungry. Lowe exploded, grabbed a loaded musket, and fired at the captain. He missed him and instead killed another crewman with a shot in the throat.

LOWTHER AND LOWE: A DEMOCRATIC DUO

Up to now, Lowe had worked on the right side of the law. But this changed after he was forced off the ship, together with his gang, and stole a small sloop that they discovered at anchor off the coast of Rhode Island. One of the sloop's crew was killed before Lowe took possession. There and then, all 13 men turned pirate. Their mood was malevolent, for as *The New York Times* article of 1892 recorded, they were determined to "make a black flag and declare war against all the world."

Lowe and his gang of 12 began by lurking around the shipping route that led from Boston to New York. This route was in frequent use by traders, virtually guaranteeing high-quality plunder. Within a few days, they had seized a Rhode Island sloop. After thoroughly pillaging the ship, the pirates cut down the rigging, making it difficult, if not impossible, for the ship to sail back to harbor and raise the alarm. The pirates' next victims were several unarmed merchantmen.

After this, Lowe headed south to the Grand Cayman islands in the Caribbean, where he encountered George Lowther, another pirate captain but one who was somewhat more experienced than himself. Lowe and Lowther decided to team up and go a-pirating together around the Caribbean islands. They were a good match for each other. Like Lowe, Lowther became famous for his skill at torture. He turned pirate in 1721 after masterminding a mutiny onboard the slave ship *Gambia Castle*, where he was second mate. The same year, Lowther and his

Lowe was profoundly affected by the death of his wife and son, and later on, as a pirate chief, he was always reluctant to hire married men for his crews.

AS THE CAPTAIN AND CREW SHALL THINK FIT
Surprisingly, perhaps, Edward Lowe and George Lowther—both fiendishly cruel, both prone to resort to terror and torture—accepted Articles of Agreement that emphasized democracy to a greater extent than anyone else's. Of the 10 conditions that made up the Lowe and Lowther Articles, half featured punishments that should be imposed as "the captain and the majority of the company shall think fit." All of them dealt with the crimes that most mattered to pirates and caused the worst ill-feeling aboard a ship full of violent, touchy, and murderous men, whose first instinct was to attack and kill an opponent rather than negotiate with him.

pirates were cruising off the Carolinas in *Happy Delivery* (*Gambia Castle* renamed) when they captured a British pirate hunter, HMS *Greyhound*. Lowther and his crew are said to have slaughtered everyone onboard before setting the ship on fire. Quite probably, by the time he encountered Lowther, Lowe had already drawn up his Articles of Agreement, for it was before their meeting that Philip Ashton was mistreated over his refusal to join Lowe's crew and sign his pirate code of conduct. George Lowther was willing to make Lowe's code his own and later on, the Articles were identified with both of them. They were also used separately when the two pirate captains parted company—amicably—in May of 1722, after some five months of mutually profitable activity. The Articles,

Edward Lowe who was feared, even by his crew, as a brute and a torturer, is shown enduring wild and windy weather while a ship that has run onto the shore appears in the background.

as published in *The Boston Newsletter*, began with the arrangements for apportioning plunder, and then went on to state:

> He that shall be found guilty of taking up any unlawful weapon on board (ship) or any other prize by us taken, so as to strike or abuse one another in any regard, shall suffer what punishment the captain and the majority of the company shall see fit.

The same applied, too, to the next three provisions: for crewmen found guilty of cowardice in battle; for failing to deliver to the Quartermaster within 24 hours any gold, jewels, silver, or other valuables discovered onboard ship; and for gaming or defrauding fellow shipmates.

In the next, sixth, provision, the compensation rate for pirates who lost a limb in battle was set at 600 pieces of eight and the seventh stated that "good quarters shall be given when craved." There was a special reward of the "best pistol or small arm" for the crew member who was the first to see a sail at sea, so alerting everyone else onboard that a prize was in prospect.

Crewmen found drunk during a battle featured in the ninth provision, the last in which punishment was decided by the "captain and the majority of the company." Their verdict was bound to be a harsh one, for the importance of staying sober at such

times could not be overemphasized. Even one incapacitated man could critically reduce the crew's ability to defend the ship. A case in point was the death of Bartholomew Roberts in 1722 (*see* page 85): by the time that HMS *Swallow* appeared and opened fire, many of his crew had drunk themselves stupid. The tenth and last provision in the Lowe and Lowther code forbade the "snaping (firing) of guns in the hold," another very important precaution for the safety of the ship and its crew.

TIME TO PART COMPANY

During their months together securing prizes and enriching themselves, Edward Lowe and George Lowther were very successful. But it was in the nature of pirate captains to prefer making their own decisions and taking their own initiatives rather than consult with a partner—or, due to the Articles of Agreement, with his crew. It was just as well that Lowe and Lowther decided to to part company

It is commonly believed that pirates were sometimes punished by being made to "walk the plank"—blindfolded and with their arms bound. In fact, there is no proof that such a punishment was ever used.

before the inevitable occurred and their egos clashed. Lowe took one of their joint prizes, the six-gun brigantine *Rebecca* with a crew of 44, and sailed north. Within a month, the pirates came upon 13 fishing vessels anchored at Port Roseway in Nova Scotia. In a bloodless coup, Lowe raised the Jolly Roger on *Rebecca*'s masthead. He informed the fishermen that there would be no quarter if any of them resisted, and forced their immediate surrender.

Every fishing boat was plundered and Lowe appropriated the largest of them, an 88-ton (80-tonne), 10-gun schooner, for himself, renaming it *Fancy*. Having abandoned the *Rebecca*, the *Fancy* became his flagship, but not for long. Lowe moved east across the Atlantic and reached the Azores, which was Portuguese territory. There, he seized a one-time man-o'-war, which he refitted, rearmed, and renamed the *Rose Pink*. *Rose Pink* became Lowe's new flagship. The Azores also yielded another prize, an English ship with two Portuguese passengers aboard. This provided Lowe with an opportunity to display his penchant for cruelty. He ordered his crew to sling them up from the yard arm, then repeatedly crash them down onto the deck until they died.

Several captured, and thoroughly pillaged, prizes later, Lowe committed a further atrocity on January 25, 1723 after he seized a Portuguese ship, the *Nostra Signoria de Victoria*. This promised to be a magnificent prize. But the Portuguese captain greatly reduced the *Victoria*'s value by throwing overboard a bag containing some 11,000 gold moidores, worth around £15,000. Lowe went incandescent with rage, sliced off the captain's lips with his cutlass and, after boiling them, forced the poor man to eat them while they were still hot. That done, Lowe ordered his pirates to kill the rest of the crew. Even Lowe's men were disgusted. One called him "a maniac and a brute."

On June 10, 1723, when Lowe was cruising in the Carolinas, the Royal Navy caught up with him. HMS *Greyhound*, a heavily armed man-o'-war, had been detailed to hunt Lowe down. Upon recognizing the pirate ship, the crew weighed in with all guns firing. But though the pirates were thrashed in the ensuing hour-long battle, Lowe and some of his men managed to escape onboard the *Fancy* and head back to the Azores. After that, sightings of Lowe reported him variously off the North American coast, the Canary Islands off the northwest coast of Africa, and off Guinea, in West Africa. From there, Lowe disappeared from view, though there were rumours placing him in Brazil or at the bottom of the ocean after his ship sank in a storm. One story claimed that he was put on trial and hanged on the French-ruled Caribbean island of Martinique. Another had it that Lowe was never caught but died in Brazil. Whatever the truth, Lowe was never seen again.

> **Lowe went incandescent with rage, sliced off the captain's lips with his cutlass and, after boiling them, forced the poor man to eat them while they were still hot.... Even Lowe's men were disgusted.**

DANGEROUS AND DUE FOR DESTRUCTION

It seems likely that, apart from his innate sadism, Edward Lowe committed atrocities in order to terrify his potential victims and persuade them to surrender quickly. However that may be, Lowe created such a ferocious image for himself that he came to the attention of the Royal Navy and its pirate-hunters. There were numerous other pirate chiefs at large in and around the Atlantic and the Caribbean, but the Navy earmarked Lowe as particularly dangerous and due for destruction.

His legacy was to remind governments how vital it was for the Atlantic shipping lanes to be patrolled and monitored on a regular basis.

LOWTHER MEETS HIS MAKER

When Lowther parted from Lowe, he commanded a single ship, *Revenge*, but forced the surrender of several vessels. He ran into trouble when attempting to take a well-armed vessel, the *Amy*, whose crew fired several broadsides at the *Revenge*, wreaking such severe damage that captain and crew had to beach their vessel and escape into the hinterland. No one from the *Amy* came after them, so they were able to spend the winter ashore repairing their ship. In the spring of 1723, Lowther set out for Newfoundland, where he seized a couple of ships, then turned south, heading for the warmer climes of the Caribbean. Once there, he sought out a suitable sheltered island where the *Revenge* could be safely careened. He found what he wanted—or thought he had—in the tiny island of Blanquilla, near Tortuga northwest of Haiti. Blanquilla was well hidden, but

Some codes made it uncomfortable for pirates to drink onboard ships, by confining them to the decks. Drinking was a perilous habit since, in battle, a drunken pirate endangered his ship and its crew.

Lowther's mistake was to choose an island too small to afford shelter from attack. The crew went ashore with the guns and provisions and the careening commenced. It was almost finished when a Royal Navy sloop, the *Eagle*, came into view. The commander, Walter Moore, recognized the *Revenge* and put a party ashore to arrest Lowther and his pirates. Lowther, a cabin boy, and three crewmen thought they had a chance to get away, and ran for it. But Blanquilla was too tiny for them to get far and there was nowhere they could hide. The crewmen and cabin boy were quickly apprehended but, at first, it seemed that Lowther had disappeared. A while later, the search party from the *Eagle* found him. He was lying in a secluded spot along the beach, an empty pistol in his hand and a bullet in his brain. Was it murder? Suicide? An accident? The truth was never discovered. But at least Captain Moore of the *Eagle* could content himself with the thought that one more pirate chief was gone, never again to infest the Atlantic shores and islands of America.

97

chapter 5

THE BRETHREN OF THE COAST

It was only 25 miles (40km) long and 70 miles (181km) square but, in the middle of the seventeenth century, the tiny West Indian island of Tortuga, off the northwest coast of Hispaniola, became a major focus of pirate activity and the operational base for the loose confederation known as the Brethren of the Coast. Many of these Brethren, who adopted their name in around 1640, were privateers. Others were pirates.

The Brethren certainly started something big because their era, which lasted from around 1640–84, led onto the so-called Golden Age of Piracy. In any case, piracy had never disappeared entirely, but underwent a big upsurge once again in the early eighteenth century, when the buccaneers of the Caribbean were being squeezed out of their hunting grounds by highly efficient and very determined pirate-hunters. This pressure forced them to seek fresh fields along the American coast, the west coast of Africa, and in the Indian Ocean.

FAMOUS PIRATES

The most famous pirates of all flourished in the 90 years or so when the Brethren and the Golden Age made them the scourge of the seas and their coastlines. They also provided the material for the writers of adventure stories, who converted some of the most vile, disreputable, real-life villains, thieves,

Drawn up alongside, these pirates are fighting their way onto the ship, using cutlasses to counter the muskets of the defenders.

cut throats and killers of all time into fierce but somehow lovable, even amusing characters of fiction. The conversion began with *Treasure Island*, the adventure novel written in 1883 by the Scots author Robert Louis Stevenson (1850–94) and its chief character, the hard-drinking, hard-swearing Long John Silver. This glamorization of the pirate continued in the work of another Scots writer, the novelist and dramatist J.M. Barrie (1860–1937). Barrie enhanced the pirate legend still further with his play *Peter Pan* (1904), which featured the evil, yet fascinating, pirate chief, Captain Hook.

Pirates continue to be popularized today through computer games, costumes, toys, T-shirts, and the latest of numerous pirate films, the Walt Disney trilogy *Pirates of the Caribbean* (2003–07). Real-life piracy was, of course, not nearly as romantic as the sanitized motion-picture versions. Even so, the makers of *Pirates of the Caribbean* did link up with reality when they based the code used in the film on the Articles of Agreement developed by the Brethren of the Coast and later adopted, with some additions, during the Golden Age as the Custom of the Coast. The code, and abiding by it, was meant to ensure that all pirates got a fair deal when it came to dividing booty, though it was also intended to curtail their natural inclination toward violence and greed.

Another important document in this context

The one-legged Long John Silver, with his crutch. Long John was a principal character in *Treasure Island* by Robert Louis Stevenson, published in 1883. Characters like Long John set the popular image of pirates.

PIRATE OR PRIVATEER?

Telling pirates and privateers apart was not always easy. The difference between them was often blurred, not least by the privateer captains, who might turn pirate for those occasions when the booty was so great that they wanted to claim all of it themselves. But charges of piracy against privateers could also be politically motivated. The Spaniards, for example, habitually labeled privateers as pirates once their treasure fleets or their settlements in America had been attacked, pillaged, and reduced to ashes.

was the Letter of Marque and Reprisal, which privateers received from the British, French, and other authorities. Letters of Marque permitted privateers to behave like pirates and hunt down, plunder, or destroy enemy vessels and their crews. But, unlike pirates, they did so under the protection of the authorities, who had, effectively, "legalized" their activities in order to claim a share of the plunder they brought home. For governments, Letters of Marque and Reprisal offered a cheap-to-run asset for waging war against their foes because, as their job description indicated, privateer captains normally owned their ships and also paid their own expenses.

THE HUNTING GROUND OF THE BRETHREN

The Caribbean, the site of a large number of the coastal colonies that made up the Spanish Main, was the chief hunting ground for the Brethren of the Coast. Here, both pirates and privateers were regularly in action in what was a veritable hotbed of international rivalry. The Spaniards and Portuguese had been first comers in America and naturally grabbed the best prizes. They were, however, challenged by would-be gatecrashers, the British, French, and Dutch, who sought to claim their share of the phenomenal riches to be found in this part of the world. The major targets were the Spanish possessions in the Americas, which had been established in the wake of discoveries by Christopher Columbus (1451–1506) in and after 1492. The Spaniards made tremendous efforts to keep their possessions secure and fend off their rivals, but they were not the only players. The British, French, and Dutch also squabbled for possession of some of the Caribbean islands and for the fortunes in booty which the Brethren of the Coast and others were able to capture by means of coastal raids and the seizure of rich cargoes at sea.

But the Brethren did not use the island of Tortuga as just another base. It was also their refuge and became so through a sequence of events that began when King Philip II of Spain (1527–98) banned foreigners from trading with the settlements of his extensive American empire. Religion as well as commerce was involved here, for at this time the dispute between Roman Catholics and breakaway Protestants was at its height.

King Philip, a Roman Catholic, was particularly anxious to exclude Protestant foreigners like the English and the Dutch, although the French, despite being fellow Catholics, were not welcome, either. But there was too much going against Philip's bid to establish the monopoly he wanted. For a start, the colonists

The pirate Captain Hook, was the deadly enemy of Peter Pan in J.M. Barrie's novel. The Captain's right hand, cut off by Peter and eaten by a crocodile, was replaced by a hook.

themselves wanted the goods that the pirates could provide because their prices were far below those charged by Spanish traders. But probably the most serious dent in Philip's attempt to keep his colonies to himself was the moves made by foreigners to plant settlements close to certain Spanish territories.

The first of these incursions took place in 1562, when French settlers set up a colony in Florida. This was followed two years later by a second at Fort Caroline, now Jacksonville. Caroline was intended as a refuge for Protestant Huguenots, who were being greviously persecuted in France. That in itself was enough to make the fort a special target for the Spaniards. They attacked in 1565, killing all of its non-Catholic defenders, and then built their own settlement at St Augustine. The English made their first incursion by planting a colony at Jamestown in Virginia in 1607, and in 1620 established themselves on the Caribbean island of St Kitts, where they were within easy reach of other, Spanish, islands and the coastal settlements of the Spanish Main, around the Caribbean Sea.

One example of Spanish savagery in defending their territory was contained in a letter written in 1604 by the Venetian ambassador in London:

Johnny Depp (left) and Orlando Bloom (with cutlass, right) featured in *The Pirates of the Caribbean* made by Walt Disney Pictures, which was based on a pirate ride at Disneyland theme parks.

The Spanish in the West Indies captured two English vessels. They cut off the hands, feet, noses and ears of the crews and smeared them with honey and tied them to trees to be tortured by flies and other insects.

Even this barbarous treatment failed to keep foreign intruders away from Spanish America. The traders had the nerve to base themselves on Hispaniola, one of Columbus's discoveries in 1492. Subsequently, Hispaniola became the jumping-off point for spreading Spanish rule into other Caribbean islands and mainland settlements in Mexico, Peru, Guatemala, and other territories of Central and South America. Once the major prizes had been secured (Aztec Mexico after 1521 and Inca Peru by 1536), the Spaniards on Hispaniola left in large numbers for the greater wealth and opportunity to be found on the mainland. In time, they were replaced on Hispaniola by the French and the English who, by the middle of the seventeenth century, were already active as privateers and pirates, preying chiefly on the treasure ships carrying vast fortunes in precious metals and jewels across the Atlantic to Spain. They were so ferocious and so diligent that they soon became known as the "nightmare of Spanish seamen." Despite this, the Spaniards were determined to expel the foreigners. They met fierce resistance, however, and had to attack the foreign settlements on Hispaniola on several occasions. At last, the French, English, and other foreigners were dislodged from the island. But they did not go a long way, venturing only as far as Tortuga, which had been settled by the French in 1625. There, the pirates and privateers soon recovered from the shock of defeat and expulsion, and before long they were once more sailing out to sea to seize and plunder Spanish vessels. The newcomers built themselves a fort and settled down to island life, although they had to live in the shadow of possible assault as the Spaniards tried a further three times to expel them from the island.

The French and English…were so ferocious and diligent that they soon became known as the "nightmare of the Spanish seamen."

JEAN LE VASSEUR

Eventually, the contest was settled, if only for a while, by Jean le Vasseur (died 1653), a French engineer from St Kitts. This was an island that had changed hands many times and was now ruled by a French nobleman, Governor-General Phillipe de Longvilliers de Poincy (1583–1660). Le Vasseur left to serve on Tortuga as its governor and brought with him a force of some 100 soldiers, including a number of pirates. He made short work of the English settlers, who were soon expelled, and then took steps to fend off more Spanish raids by building a fort overlooking the harbor.

Le Vasseur chose as his site a flat-topped hill backed by a steep rock some 30ft (9m) high. Terraces were shaped into the hillside, each of them capable of holding several hundred defenders. A curved stairway reached halfway up the rock with ladders provided for the ascent from there to the top. A natural spring provided water. Le Vasseur built a palatial home for himself on top of the rock, which also housed several cannon and storehouses for ammunition. The fort was virtually impregnable, just as le Vasseur meant it to be. Shortly after it was finished, it passed a stern test when a force of 500 Spaniards from Hispaniola attempted to destroy it. A rout followed. The fort's guns sank one of the Spanish ships and sent the rest scurrying away. The Spaniards had to land some distance

King Philip II of Spain, who struggled long and hard to keep foreign traders—and especially pirates—away from the rich Spanish colonies in the Americas. But the British, French, and Dutch thwarted him.

from the harbor, only to succumb to an ambush in which about 200 of them were killed. The remainder fled back aboard their surviving ships and sailed back to Hispaniola and safety.

At this, le Vasseur's reputation as a tough, successful leader spread far and rapidly. Before long, Tortuga was regarded as the pirate capital of the Caribbean. Le Vasseur ruled his island like a pirate-king, amassing a huge fortune in jewels and treasure—his cut from the mass of booty brought to Tortuga by its resident pirates and privateers. Even more loot reached le Vasseur's coffers by way of the

AUTHOR EXQUEMELIN EXPOSES HIS PIRATE COLLEAGUES

Alexander Exquemelin (c.1645–1707) sailed with various pirate captains. In *The Buccaneers of America*, published in 1699, he describes the behavior of one of his masters, who tended to make himself sozzled with drink, becoming prone to an excess of bonhomie:

> My own master would buy...a whole pipe of wine and placing it in the street, would force everyone that passed by to drink with him, threatening also to pistol them in case they would not do it. At other times, he would do the same with barrels of ale or beer and very often, with both hands, he would throw these liquors about the streets and wet the clothes of such as walking by without regarding whether he spoiled their apparel or not, were they men or women.

taxes he imposed on animal hides imported from Hispaniola. For the pirate community, Tortuga was evidently the place to be. Miscreants and malcontents of all kinds also regarded the island as a haven and flocked there to evade the law. In addition, the island was a place where there was so much money and treasure that pirates could fritter away their loot in a very short time. There were any number of dens of iniquity, including gaming halls, brothels, and taverns, and some pirates are known to have managed to squander up to 3000 pieces of eight in a single night.

Le Vasseur was no puritan and doubtless took such riotous behavior as a mark of success and an encouragement to other pirates to come to Tortuga and seek the fortune they were virtually certain to find. But the governor also had his less permissive side. He was, in reality, a despot through and through, and his rule over Tortuga was savage and intolerant. One of his additions to his hilltop stronghold was an iron cage, nicknamed "Little Hell," in which prisoners could neither lie down, nor stand nor sit. Likely candidates for the cage were Roman Catholics or their priests, whose services were banned by le Vasseur.

Le Vasseur was more subtle when dealing with the homosexual practices on Tortuga. He drafted in several prostitutes to keep the Tortugans on the "right" side of sexual proclivity. Even so, the governor was not above breaking one of the other rules of sexual relations. He enraged one of his lieutenants, a man called Tibuat, by stealing his mistress and then mistreating her. Revenge was due. One day in 1653, Tibuat and another lieutenant, Martin, accompanied le Vasseur when he inspected a warehouse. As soon as they got him alone inside the warehouse, Tibuat and Martin shot le Vasseur with a musket, then finished him off with daggers.

Although the aggrieved Tibuat would never have agreed, le Vasseur was a boon to both pirates and privateers. Perhaps they saw in him a fellow hardliner, who was not afraid of barbarity when it suited him. However that may be, le Vasseur's despotic regime meant a roaring trade for the pirates. They lay in wait close to the shipping routes around Tortuga and Hispaniola and thoroughly plundered any ship that fell into their hands. They invaded Hispaniola and made off with a mass of provisions from hog farms. While they were at it, the pirates sacked the small coastal towns and villages on the island, and also made

As soon as they got him alone inside the warehouse, Tibuat and Martin shot le Vasseur with a musket, then finished him off with daggers.

damaging raids on larger targets such as Santiago de los Cabaleros in eastern
Hispaniola, which they attacked in 1650. Tortuga became a thriving market for
traders, who bartered pirate plunder for guns, gunpowder, and other
ammunition, as well as brandy and cloth. French and Dutch ships were soon
making regular calls at the island to take advantage of this very lucrative trade.

A SECRET SOCIETY

On Tortuga, the Brethren of the Coast were something of a self-styled elite.
Whether they were pirates or privateers, they behaved very much like a secret
society. Except for married men, the use of surnames was forbidden, probably in
an attempt to hide the Brethrens' identities from the law. Not that the Brethren
recognized any established law. Theirs was a law that resided in a strict code
called the Custom of the Coast. Once a man had signed it, no national law
applied to him. The Brethren also superstitiously held that they could sever

**Fort Caroline in Florida
was built in 1564 by the
French to protect their
settlements from Spanish
attacks. The Fort lasted a
year before the Spaniards
destroyed it.**

Christopher Columbus, (foreground, third from the left) landed on the island of Hispaniola during his first voyage to the Americas in 1492. Subsequently, Hispaniola became a jumping-off point for Spanish conquests on the mainland.

The Brethren superstitiously held that they could sever themselves from their former life by "drowning" it as they crossed the Tropic of Cancer.

themselves from their former life by "drowning" it as they crossed the Tropic of Cancer, the northern latitude that runs south of Florida. Very conveniently, this area between the Tropic of Cancer and the equator to the south encompassed all the chief targets of the Caribbean pirates, as well as the sea lanes that were plied by treasure ships sailing the Atlantic to Europe.

The Brethren's code usually applied for one expedition only. The stipulations were agreed in detail before the start and, like all such documents, set out the conditions under which the crew was to sail. Although there were some unique additions, the provisions in the Custom of the Coast clearly made it the forerunner of codes later laid down by Bartholomew Roberts, John Phillips, Edward Lowe, and George Lowther. Votes for all important matters onboard came first, followed by the ban on gaming at cards or dice for money. Lights and candles were to be put out "at a reasonable hour of night" and any drinking after that time had to be done on the open deck. As in other codes, there was to be no "striking of one another on board." Weapons (pistols, cutlasses) had to be kept clean and fit for purpose. Compensation for injury was also included. So was the rule that the booty taken in a raid should be shared equally, and the provision that appeared in Bartholomew Roberts' code guaranteeing the musicians a day of rest, usually on the Sabbath. Two particularly fearsome punishments featured in the code. For anyone who defrauded the rest of the crew or deserted the ship, the sentence was marooning. Stealing from another crewman had an even more fearsome penalty, even though there was a tiny drop of mercy in it: the guilty were to have their ears and nose slit but were left on the shore of an island with inhabitants. This would mean hardship but not certain death.

This same penalty was imposed in a provision not mentioned in other pirate codes, dealing with the issue of homosexuality onboard pirate ships. Here

The Spanish Main was a necklace of Spanish settlements around the Caribbean, including not only those on the mainland but also the islands in the Caribbean Sea. The Main was the major target for pirates.

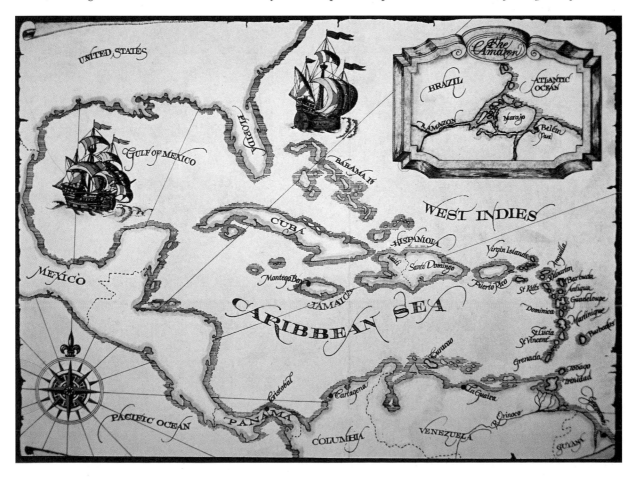

Governor le Vasseur's solution was, of course, impossible. Women were not only forbidden but their presence was believed to be unlucky. In addition, even when confined to the Caribbean, voyages involved a great deal of time at sea—too much time, in fact. A journey of 1988 miles (3200km) from Barbados to Havana, in Cuba, for example, could take as much as 36 days. The 995 miles (1600km) between Barbados and Tortuga occupied 18 days. These were not always days of furious activity. At times, a pirate or privateer ship could search the Caribbean for weeks on end without sighting any prey. This meant crews could have a lot of time on their hands and not very much to do with it. So, according to the Custom of the Coast, punishment awaited "any person...found seducing another" and "if either were to keep it from the crew, then both shall be set on shore" in an inhabited place to face whatever hardships that involved.

"TO SEEK THEIR DESPERATE FORTUNES"

Once the Brethren had agreed and signed up to their Custom of the Coast, they got together to decide where their theater of operations was going to be or, as they put it, where they were to "seek their desperate fortunes." In their early days, in the middle of the seventeenth century, the Brethren of the Coast used to choose their leader from their own ranks, but later on, the man who owned the ship and was himself an experienced pirate had an obvious right to be captain. Even so, he had to be on his best behavior throughout a voyage because the critical eyes of the crew were always upon him. If by any chance he proved to be unsatisfactory and failed to perform his duties properly, he could be deprived of his post. Unlike ships of the Royal Navy and similar vessels of other nations, removing the captain of a pirate vessel did not, apparently, count as mutiny.

Young boys onboard a pirate ship or privateer had a particular task in certain circumstances. Pirates were always looking for a better vessel with, perhaps, better armament or more spacious accommodation. If a captured prize turned out to be superior to their own, the boys would set fire to their own ship and transfer, with the whole crew, to the prize.

However random or spontaneous such proceedings may seem, a pirate or privateering expedition was very tightly organized. The first order of business was to decide how to provision the ship. For some time, the hog farms on Hispaniola provided them with pork, which was the pirates' staple food. Some of these farms contained a thousand hogs or more, which meant that one raid could provide victuals for the whole expedition. The pirates attacked the big hogyards at night. Waking the guard, they threatened him with death if he dared disobey their orders or make a noise. Then they emptied the farm buildings of hogs and carried them back to their ship to be butchered and salted for their meat. The next source of food to be exploited was the turtles that proliferated in the waters around Tortuga, the name of which actually translates as "turtle."

A popular delicacy was the meat of the manatee, a marine mammal 3ft (1m) long, plentiful in the Caribbean and the Gulf of Mexico. With an average adult weight of up to 1200lb (544kg), the manatee was large enough to keep a pirate crew very well fed for quite some time. There were two meals a day onboard a pirate ship and the men were allowed to eat as much as they wanted.

Some time before putting out to sea, everyone concerned with the voyage was advised of the day they were expected to embark. Each crewman was informed of

At times, a pirate or privateer ship could search the Caribbean for weeks on end without sighting any prey. This meant crews could have a lot of time on their hands and not very much to do with it.

the amount of powder and bullets he should bring with him to cover any actions that might take place during the voyage. Another way of gathering a crew for a pirate expedition reflected the fame of particular pirate leaders like Henry Morgan, Edward Mansfield (died 1667), or the French pirate Michel de Grammont (*c*.1645–86). Men like these were the superstars of seventeenth-century piracy, and their names and achievements were well known throughout the Caribbean. Consequently, pirates scrambled to serve under them because they appeared to have some magic touch that guaranteed success. All Morgan and the others had to do was announce that they were "going on account" and name the meeting place. Scores of would-be crewmen would emerge from every island and bay in close proximity, carrying their own short swords or flintlocks.

Naturally, not every "brother of the Coast" was able to draw on this level of enthusiasm, but those who could usually did so by way of spectacular achievement. One pirate chief of this caliber was Bartholomew Sharpe (1650–*c*.1690) who, with other Brethren of the Coast, crossed the Isthmus of Panama early in 1680. Once there, they spent some 18 months seizing and plundering Spanish ships and towns along the Pacific coast of South America, enriching themselves all the way. Sharpe's greatest prize was the Spanish

Turtles were an important source of food for both the native tribes in the northern Caribbean and for the pirates. Tortuga meant "turtle," which gave its name to the island.

111

treasure ship *La Santissima Trinidad*, which he captured while she was on her way to Panama City from Callao, the port of Lima, in Peru. The *Trinidad* contained huge wealth in silver plate, pieces of eight, fruit, oil, and jars of wine as well as one unique prize of inestimable value. This was a copy of an atlas containing sea charts and maps that recorded the positions of all the ports, water depths, creeks, rivers, capes, and coasts that guided Spanish sea captains sailing the "South Seas," the Pacific and Indian oceans south of the equator.

With this, vital secrets that the Spaniards had been determined to keep to themselves were revealed. On his return to Britain in 1681, Bartholomew Sharpe handed the atlas to the king, Charles II (1630–85). It was a canny move: the atlas saved his life. King Charles admired adventurers like Sharpe, who were willing to take great risks and had the impudence to get away with it. It seems possible that Charles used his influence to secure an acquittal for Sharpe after he was indicted on charges of murder and piracy. Either of these crimes was liable to the death penalty, but Sharpe was let off with a modest fine of eight shillings and four pence. In addition, Sharpe was offered the command of the Royal Navy sloop *Bonetta*. However, a steady job in government service was not for him. He preferred his independence and a life of adventure on the high seas. Refusing the offer, he returned to the Caribbean. There, as far as is known, he continued pirating until he died, aged around 40, in 1690.

JOHN COXON

Other Brethren who also took part in the mass raid along the Pacific coast of South America included John Coxon (died 1689), whose 88-ton (80-tonne) ship carried eight guns and a crew of 97 men. Coxon was based at Porto Bello in Jamaica, which had been ruled by Britain since 1670. He first came to prominence in 1677, when he plundered Santa Marta on the Caribbean coast of Colombia. In addition to booty, he carried off the town's governor and bishop—presumably to hold for ransom. Coxon's next exploit was a raid in the Gulf of Honduras, which yielded money and plate, as well as 500 chests of indigo dye, cocoa, cochineal, and tortoiseshell—all valuable booty. At Panama in 1680, Coxon captured an entire fleet of men-o'-war. On occasion, he disguised himself as a privateer after stealing Letters of Marque and Reprisal belonging to another pirate-chief, Robert Clarke, who was hanged in around 1709 for "treason."

Privateers like Sharpe and Coxon were the heavyweights among the Brethren of the Coast, thinking big and acting extravagantly. However, by the time John

There was a big market for "pirate wood," as it was sometimes called, on the English-ruled island of Jamaica, much to the fury of the Spaniards, whose forests in Mexico were being poached.

PERILS OF THE PIRATE LIFESTYLE

The extreme dangers faced by pirates, whether at sea or onshore, and the arduous nature of expeditions were making them wonder if the freedom, the comradeship, the fair shares guaranteed under the pirate code, the plenteous food, and the wealth they stood to gain were really worth having. Few pirates survived into middle or old age: 40 years or thereabouts was the limit for many of them. There had to be a better, more secure way of making a living, and by the later years of the seventeenth century, an increasing number of pirates were setting out to find it.

Coxon captured his extraordinary haul at Panama, the situation in the Caribbean was changing—and in ways that made piracy look like an increasingly poor life choice for many pirates.

On Tortuga, pirates began to look to the copious forests to provide log-wood. This they could cut and sell to other Caribbean islands. Neighboring Hispaniola furnished valuable woods and when that source ran out, as it eventually did, the woods and forests of the Yucatán peninsula in Mexico were an easy target to exploit. There was a big market for "pirate wood," as it was sometimes called, on the English-ruled island of Jamaica, much to the fury of the Spaniards, whose forests in Mexico were being poached.

The Spanish protested about this highly profitable trade in wood, but their complaints fell on deaf ears. So, in

French buccaneer Michel de Grammont targeted Spanish shipping in the Caribbean and Spanish towns in Venezuela and Mexico.

113

Caca Fogo.   Caca Plata.

Pirates attacking a ship. The pirate ship maneuvered close to its victim to give it no chance of getting away and to enable the pirate crew to board and plunder it.

an attempt to put a stop to it, they resorted to hiring pirates of their own. It was a move that failed. The ex-pirates adopted a convoy system, by which their trading vessels sailed in company, thus offering each other protection. Meanwhile, the trade with Jamaica continued. Worse still for the Spaniards, ex-pirates and other foreign traders began to settle on the coast of Hispaniola and other areas around the Gulf of Mexico, including Honduras and Guatemala. Both were Spanish possessions and both were marketplaces for trading with the Dutch, who brought the settlers important benefits and much profit. They were able to exchange their tobacco and ginger for the goods brought by the Dutch to America, including African slaves.

THE IMPUDENT DUTCH

The Dutch were a particular pest for the Spaniards. Until 1581, when the Dutch in the northern part of The Netherlands declared their independence, their territory had been a Spanish possession. Spain had conquered the greatest overseas empire then existing in the world, and was unwilling to admit that it had lost to a feisty but minor new nation, so it was not until 1648 that the Spaniards could bring themselves to acknowledge the free status of The Netherlands. Just over 20 years later, the Spaniards were still smarting from the shame when they had to confront the Dutch in their American colonies. Their lack of success was salt in a recently inflicted wound.

The French had better luck. In 1665, a new French governor, Bertrand Denis d'Ogeron (1615–75), arrived on Tortuga. Trading with the Dutch was still continuing at that time, but d'Ogeron gradually began to reduce contact by sending out regular squadrons of frigates to police the local waters and drive the Dutch away. Afterward, d'Ogeron hired privateers and pirates from Tortuga and Hispaniola to back up French forces as they attempted to trounce the Spaniards and expand French power in the Caribbean.

Despite this, the pirates and privateers on Tortuga never really trusted d'Ogeron and he never entirely controlled them. Consequently, Tortuga remained a base for pirate forays out into the Caribbean, where they continued raiding foreign vessels and foreign colonies, and the colonies of Spain in particular. But the efforts of d'Ogeron and even those of the Spaniards did have some effect by reducing the blithe freedom with which the pirates had once conducted their illicit business. Some aspiring privateers took the precaution of obtaining French commissions for their expeditions. Even the famous Welsh privateer and one of the most famous of the Brethren of the Coast, Sir Henry Morgan (c.1635–88) felt obliged to conceal his activities under Letters of Marque from the French. This was a precaution he took in 1670 before setting sail with 500 pirates from Tortuga and another 1500 from Jamaica to plunder and terrorize Panama, Maracaibo, and Puerto Bello on the coast of Venezuela, together with Santa Marta in Colombia and Moskito in Nicaragua.

> But the efforts of d'Ogeron and even those of the Spaniards did have some effect by reducing the blithe freedom with which the pirates had once conducted their illicit business.

PIRATE STRONGHOLD AT MARACAIBO

Eight years later, in 1678, the French pirate Michel de Grammont gave an even more resounding display of defiance to the Spanish powers-that-be in America. In June of that year, de Grammont sailed for Maracaibo with crews numbering some 1000 men and captured and plundered the town. He went on to attack and pillage the Spanish settlements around Maracaibo, setting up a pirate stronghold as a center of operations. It lasted for the next six months. Meanwhile, more pirates under the command of a French aristocrat, the Marquis de Maintenon (1648–91), were also ravaging the Venezuelan coast. Their other targets were the pearl fisheries at Margarita Island in Venezuela and Spanish settlements on Trinidad. Morgan, Grammont, and Maintenon were lionized for their daring raids and the lavish prizes they produced, but the reality was that their days of piracy

King Charles II admired daring rascals like Henry Morgan, whom he saved from being sent to trial for piracy after his raid on Panama in 1670. Three years later, Charles rewarded Morgan with a knighthood.

were almost over. The collusion between Britain or France and the Brethren of the Coast had been a mutually agreeable and very profitable arrangement. But as time went on, the combination of dirty politics on the one hand and brute materialism on the other became less and less compatible with colonial ambitions. Both Britain and France were moving out of the phase when infuriating and robbing Spain, Portugal, and each other constituted foreign policy. Instead, they were looking to the long term when they would have to live together as empire builders, trading with each other and using diplomacy to resolve their differences.

THE EFFECTS OF COLONIZATION

Despite Spanish efforts to close off America to Protestants and other intruders, British, French, and Dutch colonization in the Caribbean was already under way in the seventeenth century. Spain retained the major share of American colonies, but Britain, France, and The Netherlands were fast acquiring much of the rest. Britain added the Caribbean islands of Barbados (1628), Montserrat (1632), and Antigua (1632) to St Kitts (1623), and took over St Lucia (1663). In 1666, it acquired Nassau in the Bahama Islands and in 1684 claimed Bermuda. France acquired Martinique and Guadeloupe in 1635 and, after some tussling with the British, French Guiana on the northern coast of South America, in 1667. The Dutch took Curaçao (1634) and Aruba (1647), in what are now the Netherlands Antilles, to use as adjuncts to the slave trade. As this new, more ordered world developed, pirates and privateers became a liability because of their wild,

In 1669, the Welsh pirate Henry Morgan sacked Maracaibo on the Gulf of Venezuela and tortured the citizens of nearby Gibraltar to make them reveal where they had hidden their treasure.

117

unpredictable nature and their habit of going off pirating on their own behalf as and when suitable prizes presented themselves. Moreover, their activities could easily unsettle relations between countries trying to formulate a new, more grown-up way of dealing with one another.

THE TREATY OF RATISBON

The coup de grâce came in 1684, when France and Spain set aside their longstanding enmity to sign the Treaty of Ratisbon in Germany. Under the Treaty, pirates were declared to be felons. This meant that, as criminals, they could be prosecuted and, if found guilty, executed.

The 18th-century actor, Mr. Helme, famously played Blackbeard, that most fearsome of pirates—although he did not emulate the pirate's habit of using fuses to set strands of his long beard on fire.

MR. HELME AS BLACKBEARD THE PIRATE.
As Performed at the Royal Circus, Feb 10th 1799.

Although all pirates around the world were meant to be included in its provisions, the Treaty was chiefly aimed at clearing them out of the Caribbean. Rather than wait for expulsion, pirates on Tortuga began to pack up and leave the island. By 1688, they were largely gone. In England, similar moves were made against privateers: any Englishman found privateering under a national flag other than his own was committing a felony. He could not sail under the British flag either, for the British ceased issuing Letters of Marque once the Treaty came into force. In either case, the punishment was death. Some "disinherited" pirates turned pirate-hunter and aided the authorities in tracking down their former comrades. Others left the Caribbean altogether, and took up piracy in Africa, America, or the Indian and Pacific Oceans, where they hoped to escape the jurisdiction of the Treaty.

Some, though, enjoyed one last great pirate fling in the Caribbean. In 1697, they targeted the rich Spanish port of Cartagena de Indias, now in Colombia on the northwest coast of South America. Galleons at anchor in Cartagena were loaded with gold and silver from the mines in Colombia and Peru for the voyage across the Atlantic to Spain. Other vessels carried slaves. The raid of 1697 was an all-French affair, carried out by two former pirates, both latterly admirals in the French navy—Bernard Desjean, Baron de Pontis (1645–1707)—along with Jean Baptiste du Casse (1646–1715), who in 1691 had been appointed Governor of Hispaniola, now a French possession. Pontis and du Casse captured Cartagena and demanded a ransom from its citizens. The wealth they received was stunning and included a quantity of emeralds weighing more than 990lb (450kg), gold and silver bullion worth 7.5 million francs, a chestful of church silverware, and a magnificent statue of the Madonna dressed in a silver robe encrusted with precious stones. If this was not the greatest haul ever made by pirates, it came pretty close to it.

BLACKBEARD'S PIRATE REPUBLIC

The Caribbean never experienced piracy as flamboyant as the raid on Cartagena again, but the party was by no means over. The Treaty of Ratisbon may have set out the ground rules, but there was still a deal of mopping up to do. For many years, Britain's Royal Navy and the Spanish Guardacosta (coast guard) had protected their shipping and its routes with some success. But by 1700 both services had been greatly strengthened, enabling them to hit the Brethren of the Coast and other privateers and pirates much harder than before. In particular, they reduced the number of safe havens where pirates had once been able to sidle out of sight, there to resupply, repair, and rest and relax before setting out again in search of loot.

The last of these havens was in the Bahama Islands, where Edward Teach, known as Blackbeard (1680–1718), based himself at Fort Nassau. In 1700, Nassau was actually under pirate rule, Teach lording it over the "Pirate Republic" as its magistrate. It was a state of affairs that did not continue for long. In 1718, the British authorities used the poacher-turned-gamekeeper technique. They appointed a one-time privateer, Woodes Rogers (c.1679–1732) as Captain-General and Governor in Chief over the Bahama Islands. His brief was to clear out those pirates who had slipped past the Treaty of Ratisbon, continuing their nefarious activities among the islands and hiding places of the Caribbean Sea.

Under the Treaty of Ratisbon, pirates were declared to be felons. This meant that, as criminals, they could be prosecuted and if found guilty, executed.

chapter 6

TALES FROM THE CARIBBEAN

Pirates and privateers of the past are among the very few people in history to retain their fascination long after their own lifetime. More than four centuries after European navigators opened up the world to new empires, new trade, and, unavoidably, new pirates, the coasts and islands of the Caribbean still remain the centerpiece of pirate tales and lore. Men who made their names and their fortunes in the Caribbean, such as Henry Morgan or the terrifying, half-mad Blackbeard, Edward Teach, evoke images of wondrous treasure, adventure on the high seas and glamorous lives that, though often short, were far from routine. There were others, too, less well known but not necessarily less successful and with their own extraordinary tales to tell.

Christopher Myngs (1625–66), for example, was a commander in the Royal Navy, who doubled as a Caribbean pirate after he participated in a raid on Santa Marta, Venezuela. What made Myngs step aside from a promising career in the Navy is not precisely known, but five months before the raid, in January 1656, he sailed the 44-gun frigate

A pirate boat sails past the stern of a Spanish galleon. Spanish galleons or treasure ships were prize targets for pirates, for they carried an immense amount of treasure.

He might look mild and even inoffensive, but Christopher Myngs could be as brutal and as tricky as any more obviously villainous pirate and plundered with the same gusto.

Marston Moor to Jamaica. There he met several men who had tempting yarns to spin about the amazing wealth that could be made by piracy.

Myngs, who was born in Norfolk, is first mentioned in the record as the captain of the *Elisabeth* during the first Anglo–Dutch war of 1652–54, when he captured two Dutch men-o'-war and took them home as prizes. The exploit earned him promotion in the Navy. In early 1658, still serving in Jamaica, Myngs took part in the later stages of the second Anglo–Spanish War of 1655–60. During the fighting, he was accused of cruelty and of sacking entire towns, and afterward massacring the inhabitants. The ships under his command, it was claimed, were crewed not by Royal Navy personnel but by pirates.

However that may be, Myngs was now acting more like a pirate chief than a naval commander. He turned to raiding the coast of South America and in 1659, plundered three towns along the coast of Venezuela, taking a share of the proceeds amounting to $506,260 (£250,000). The raids earned Myngs the ire of the Spaniards, who proclaimed him a pirate and a mass murderer. Indeed, they made a formal complaint about Myngs to London, but he was in much deeper trouble than that. Edward d'Oyley (1617–75) the Royal Navy commander in Jamaica, had forbidden Myngs to take any bounty after the raids of 1659 and ordered his arrest for embezzlement. In 1660, Myngs was sent back on England onboard the *Marston Moor* along with a letter that described him as "unhinged and out of tune."

By the time the *Marston Moor* reached home, King Charles II had been restored to the English throne after living in exile for the 11 years of republican rule. Amnesty was in the air, particularly for such an impudent, adventurous fellow like Christopher Myngs, who was just the sort of rascal King Charles most admired. The upshot was that Myngs went unpunished and retained his

WITH FULL ROYAL KNOWLEDGE AND CONSENT
Myngs was the perfect instrument for King Charles's clandestine undermining of his foes, with his recent experience of raiding, his acquaintance with pirates and buccaneers, and his evident taste for the savage warfare that was usually involved. Myngs decided to promote a full-blooded effort by promising pirates that there would be no limit imposed on future plunder or rapine or, indeed, any other terror they inflicted on their victims. The new governor of Jamaica, Thomas Rickman, Seventh Baron Windsor of Stanwell (?1627–87) gave Myngs his full support and approval.

command. Moreover, in August of 1662, he returned to Jamaica in charge of the *Centurion,* with encouragement from the King to carry on pirating. This was not as out of order as it may seem. Governments habitually used pirates to undermine their enemies, using Letters of Marque and Reprisal to mask their underhand dealings. In this context, Christopher Myngs was being used as part of an ongoing policy to damage or destroy the infrastructure of Spain's all-embracing power in Central and South America and the Caribbean.

The Four Days' Battle took place in 1666 during the second Anglo–Dutch War. Christopher Myngs, then an admiral in the Royal Navy, took part in what turned out to be a heavy English defeat.

ASSAULT ON SANTIAGO DE CUBA

In 1662, Myngs led an assault on Santiago de Cuba in southeast Cuba, capturing the town despite its strong defenses. Its fortress was blown up and six Spanish ships were captured. This success acted as a clarion call to pirates from all over the Caribbean to join Myngs' next expedition. This time, the fleet comprised 14 ships, with around 1500 pirates onboard, and the target was San Francisco de Campeche on the Gulf of Mexico, which had been subject to pirate raids ever since it was founded by Spaniards in 1540. But Myngs' assault, in 1663, was so savage that it caused outrage in England, and King Charles was obliged to cancel plans for further attacks. Once the furor had died down, however, the attacks resumed, continuing, on and off, for another 40 years, devastating the entire area.

Henry Morgan's crew disembarks on an island, probably in the Caribbean. Pirates and buccaneers usually sought out remote and isolated islands for the safety they provided from pirate-hunters and rivals.

Myngs was badly wounded at Campeche and returned to England to recuperate. In the next two years, he rose steadily through the ranks, and by the time of the Second Anglo–Dutch War he was a vice-admiral and a knight of the realm. One of the actions in the Second War was the so-called Four Days' Battle, fought between June 1 and 4, 1666. Myngs, who was commanding a flotilla in the action, was seriously injured by a Dutch sniper while onboard his flagship *Victory*: he was shot through the cheek and left shoulder. Myngs returned to London for treatment but died soon after his arrival.

HENRY MORGAN

Among the 1500 pirates involved in the attack led by Christopher Myngs on Santiago de Cuba was Henry Morgan, then 27 years old and, according to one among the many versions of his early life, taking part in his first privateering expedition. The first document to mention him by name refers to him as Henry Morgan, captain of a ship in a fleet of 10 sailing under Letters of Marque. The plundering expeditions along the Spanish Main that followed made Morgan a rich man and also earned him the respect and admiration of buccaneers and pirates all over the Caribbean. Morgan was also fortunate enough to acquire influence in high places when his uncle, Colonel Edward Morgan (died c.1669), was appointed Lieutenant-Governor of Jamaica. Through him, Morgan gained special favors from the island government.

In 1668, when England was involved in one of its regular wars with Spain, the Jamaican government commissioned Morgan as Admiral of the Fleet in command of a large force of privateers. They launched their first attack against Puerto Principe, now known as Camagüey, in central Cuba, but the Spaniards learned about it in advance and concealed most of their treasure. All that Morgan and his privateers managed to capture was a disappointing 50,000 pieces of eight, a very modest figure considering the normal yield of such raids.

Morgan's next strike was much more lucrative and very much more extensive, for the potential of the target, Portobello on the Isthmus of Panama, was gigantic. At Portobello, the Spaniards gathered treasure brought in from the surrounding countryside—gold, silver, jewels—to embark on treasure ships bound for Spain. Needless to say, Portobello was heavily fortified. There were three forts, each

Myngs, who was commanding a flotilla in the action, was seriously injured by a Dutch sniper while on board his flagship *Victory*: he was shot through the cheek and left shoulder.

There was fighting during Morgan's first raid, on Puerto Principe, but the haul of 50,000 pieces of eight was poor compared to normal pirate booty.

garrisoned by a large contingent of soldiers. A daunting prospect, but not for Henry Morgan. Under cover of darkness he ordered his men, who were well armed, to row out in canoes and take the Spaniards by surprise. The ruse succeeded with the first two forts, but the third proved to be a problem. Morgan's men tried twice to take it, and twice failed.

Morgan, though, had not yet run through his bag of tricks. Several nuns and Jesuit priests had been captured as hostages during the fight for the first two forts. Morgan now ordered that they be lined up in front of his men, to be used as shields while his men climbed up ladders and scaled the walls of the fort. Not surprisingly, the defenders of the fort declined to fire, for fear of killing such holy personages, and so it was not long before the third fort fell into Morgan's hands.

The town of Portobello, shorn of its defenses, soon followed and was subjected to a terrible month of plunder, torture, rape, and binge-drinking before the surviving inhabitants promised Morgan a ransom of 350,000 pieces of eight. But the Spanish governor of Panama refused to hand over this extraordinary amount and instead sent a force of some 3000 troops overland to take Portobello and eject Morgan and his men. However, unknown to the Governor, the local Indians at Panama, who were implacably opposed to the Spaniards, learned of his plan and informed Morgan. As a result, the Governor's forces were ambushed before they could reach the town. Still hopeful of arranging a deal, the Governor of Panama now offered Morgan 100,000 pieces of eight. Although this was around 70 percent less than he had demanded, it was still a sizeable ransom. Morgan accepted the offer, set free the hostages, and sailed back to Jamaica and a hero's welcome.

Priests and monks could be regular victims of pirate raids since they were guardians of the lucrative wealth to be found in churches and monasteries. Here, priests plead for their lives with armed pirates.

ATTACK ON *OXFORD*

The expedition to Portobello had been such a success, despite the reduced ransom, that Morgan's crews were soon asking for more. But then came a fearful setback. Morgan was hosting a banquet for the captains of his fleet onboard

his flagship, the frigate *Oxford*, when there was a tremendous explosion. The *Oxford* was almost completely destroyed, and most of the crew were killed. Morgan, together with some of his guests, managed to survive and, it appears, took the disaster quite coolly. Now needing a ship and crew, he seized *Le Cerf Volant*, which belonged to a French pirate. Renaming her *Satisfaction*, Morgan commandeered her crew and set off to raid the town of Maracaibo on the northwest coast of Venezuela, in the Gulf of Venezuela. Morgan's reconnaissance had not been all that good, however, and he did not know that the Spaniards had recently fortified the area around Maracaibo. But being one of the more intelligent and ingenious Brethren of the Coast, he countered this unexpected problem with a Plan B. Realizing that an assault from the sea was likely to be disastrous, he approached Maracaibo from the landward side instead. The Spaniards were taken by surprise, and Morgan captured the fort.

In the next eight weeks, Morgan and his privateers stripped the inhabitants of Maracaibo of nearly $50,000 worth of jewels and silver. They then moved further along the coast to the town of Gibraltar, where Morgan had several victims tortured to force a ransom out of them. This, though, yielded only 5000 pieces of eight. Disappointed, the pirates decided to return to Jamaica, but to their alarm, they found that the entrance to Gulf of Venezuela—the only way out—was blocked by three Spanish warships. Morgan was now in serious trouble. These warships—the 40-gun flagship *Magdalena*, the 30-gun *Luis*, and the 24-gun *Marquesa*—were far more powerful than the ships of Morgan's pirate fleet, none

Henry Morgan cunningly tricked his way out of a trap when the Spaniards blocked the way out of Lake Maracaibo in 1669. Morgan escaped out into the Caribbean.

The *Oxford* was almost completely destroyed, and most of the crew were killed but Morgan...it appears, took the disaster quite coolly.

Spanish or Portuguese treasure ships, which could be loaded with huge wealth, were the most desirable targets for pirates in the Caribbean. This Spanish treasure vessel was captured, plundered, and later burned by Henry Morgan.

of which carried more than 20 guns apiece. Worse still, the Spaniards had backed their formidable fleet with a fortified island, San Carlos, which bristled with guns.

STAY AND FIGHT

Then, the Spaniards made an astounding offer. Instead of destroying the intruders, Don Alonso del Campo y Espinosa, in command of the Spanish ships, chose to be lenient. He gave Morgan and his men two days to decide whether to return their plunder to its owners and leave, or to stay and fight. The pirates voted to fight, but not in the way the Spaniards expected. Morgan ordered preparations to be made overnight and at dawn next day, the Spaniards awoke to find several small pirate vessels sailing toward them. Suspecting nothing and sure of their superiority, the Spaniards prepared to board the ship. But when it came close to the *Magdalena,* the ship exploded with a mighty roar and became a mass of leaping flames. The *Magdalena* soon caught fire, and sank. This was not the only disaster suffered by the Spaniards. The *Luis* ran aground and also sank. Then Morgan attacked and captured Don Alonso's remaining ship, the *Marquesa,* after a brief, fierce fight.

But the encounter was not yet at an end. Despite the loss of all three of his ships, Espinosa still held the whip hand, for the Spanish Vice Admiral retained command of the fort on San Carlos Island, which also blocked the only exit to the Gulf. The resourceful Morgan cracked this problem by mounting a fake attack on the fort, designed to fool the Spaniards into swiveling their guns round and away from the exit to the Gulf. The ruse succeeded. While the Spaniards and their guns were looking in the opposite direction, waiting for an attack on the fort that never came, Morgan and his fleet sailed out of the Gulf of Venezuela and escaped into the Caribbean.

Back at Port Royal, Jamaica, Morgan received more than another hero's welcome. He now possessed an unchallenged reputation for daring and for breaking records for the seizure of prize booty. Recruits virtually stampeded to be included in his next expedition, the projected sack of Panama, the most ambitious and dangerous of any previous expedition. With 900 men in nine ships, Morgan set sail once again in October 1669. But this time, Morgan's luck appeared to have deserted him. At Cartagena, the principal port of the Spanish Main, his flagship blew up after some of his men, much the worse for drink, lit candles too close to a barrel of gunpowder, killing themselves and one-third of the crew. Next, at Maracaibo and the town of Gibraltar along the coast, the inhabitants were once again forewarned of Morgan's approach and escaped, taking their treasure.

THE SACK OF PANAMA

Morgan, however, was undeterred. The following year, 1670, he returned to the Isthmus of Panama. He arrived in massive strength, commanding 36 ships and some 2000 men who had come from Port Royal, Jamaica, and Tortuga to take part in his latest expedition. First, Morgan secured the surrender of the Spanish fort at San Lorenzo, which lay at the head of the River Chagres. The river, some 600 miles (965km) long, led to the city of Panama, where the most fabulous treasure of all—houses, jewelry, and other valuables belonging to wealthy merchants, and an immense fortune in gold extracted from the Spanish colon in Peru—was waiting for them.

For the 1400 men who accompanied Morgan, getting there involved sailing up the river by canoe, followed by a two-week trek through the tropical jungle

In 1670, when Henry Morgan (sitting at the right end of the table) attacked the city of Panama, he used threats and torture to make the Spanish inhabitants reveal where they had hidden their treasure.

François de l'Olonnais was one of the most cruel and sadistic pirates operating in the Caribbean. He habitually used torture and terror and was dreaded throughout the Spanish Main.

that covered the Isthmus. Apart from its gruelling terrain, the Isthmus featured dangerous animals, and poisonous insects that carried a multiplicity of fevers and other serious diseases. Morgan and his men entered this seemingly impenetrable jungle at the beginning of January 1671. They almost starved on the way, as they had neglected to take any provisions with them. Luckily, they were saved after the first week, when they came upon a barn full of maize, which the Spaniards had failed to destroy. But Morgan's seemingly suicidal strategy had a crafty purpose. The Isthmus was considered impassable, so the Spaniards at Panama never imagined that Morgan would attack from that direction. Once again, the guns protecting Panama City, like those on San Carlos Island, were facing the wrong way. The Spaniards had no option but to come out of their defensive position and fight the invaders in the open. An exhausting two-hour battle ensued, and eventually the Spanish ranks crumbled and then fled in retreat. After another three hours, Morgan and his men captured Panama City itself.

The Sack of Panama that followed, involved three weeks of plunder, terror, and destruction, in which large areas of the city were razed to the ground. Indeed, Panama was still burning four weeks later. Morgan and his men amassed so much wealth that they needed about 175 pack mules to carry it. Each mule was laden with gold, silver, and other booty whose value was almost inestimable. Somehow, though, a rumor circulated that each man who had taken part in the Sack of Panama was going to be rewarded with only 200 pieces of eight.

At this, Henry Morgan insisted that everyone, including himself, should be strip searched. This was meant to ensure that none of them had broken the provision in the pirate code not to conceal any loot. But it seems that when the time came to return to Jamaica, Morgan was not so keen to prove himself honest. He embarked his cut of the loot aboard his ship and sailed to Port Royal, leaving his men behind. This cynical betrayal had little effect on his reputation. In both Jamaica and England, he was treated as a hero and received remarkable honors, including a knighthood from King Charles II and an appointment as Lieutenant-Governor of Jamaica, the same post once held by his uncle, Edward. After Panama, Henry Morgan never went privateering again. He lived in Jamaica for the rest of his life and died at Port Royal in 1688, the most prestigious and successful of all the Brethren of the Coast.

FRANÇOIS DE L'OLONNAIS

Morgan's opposite, the most notorious brother of the Coast, was Jean David Nau, better known as François de l'Olonnais (1630–71) after his birthplace, Olonne, on the west coast of France. Piracy and de l'Olonnais were made for each other, not simply because of the potential for gain and adventure in the pirate's life, but for the opportunities it afforded for cruelty and torture. De L'Olonnais pursued the latter on such a scale that he earned a reputation as the "Flail of the Spaniards" and "one of the most pitiless blackguards who ever cut a Spaniard's throat."

De L'Olonnais began his career as a pirate by preying and plundering along the shipping lanes that ran from the West Indies and the Spanish Main to Hispaniola. His first two or three expeditions were successful, but his luck did not hold. In 1667, his ship was wrecked on the coast of Campeche in the southwest of the Yucatán peninsula in Mexico. De L'Olonnais managed to get ashore with the remnants of his crew, only to be set upon by Spaniards. Most of the crew were slaughtered, and de l'Olonnais was wounded. He escaped, however, by smearing himself with the blood of his crewmen and playing dead. Afterwards, de l'Olonnais swore vengeance: "I shall never henceforward give quarter to any Spaniard whatsoever."

He got his chance after he captured a group of fishermen and forced them to reveal the whereabouts of the Spaniards. De l'Olonnais and his pirates attacked the next morning, swarming onboard the Spanish warship with their sharp-edged cutlasses and driving the crew below deck. The men were then ordered to come up one at a time and as each of them emerged, de l'Olonnais sliced off their heads.

Afterward, de l'Olonnais resumed pirating, with some success. One of his prizes was a ship bound for Maracaibo in the Gulf of Venezuela, carrying a fortune in money and merchandise. When de l'Olonnais saw the port, he recognized at once that it was a very fruitful target for plunder, offering a prize that justified what became one of the most powerful pirate raids ever mounted by a Brother of the Coast.

The pirate fleet, consisting of nine ships carrying 600 crew, sailed from Tortuga at the end of April 1667. On the way, de l'Olonnais captured a vessel loaded with more than 12,000lb (5400kg) of cacao beans, 40,000 pieces of eight, and jewels worth another 10,000 pieces of eight. These riches were so great that de l'Olonnais sent the ship back to Tortuga to be unloaded. Then it returned to Hispaniola, where the crew seized another vessel carrying over 6600lb (3000kg) of gunpowder, a supply of muskets, and 12,000 more pieces of eight.

Morgan embarked his cut of the loot aboard his ship and sailed to Port Royal, leaving his men behind. This cynical betrayal had little effect on his reputation. In both Jamaica and England, he was treated as a hero.

TORTURE TACTICS
De L'Olonnais used several methods to cause his victims agony. He burned some of them alive, cut out their tongues, or sliced them up slowly, bit by bit. Or he would cut open a victim's chest with his cutlass, pull out the heart, and gnaw at it with his teeth, like a ravenous animal.

After the excitement roused by such magnificent treasure, Maracaibo was an anti-climax. The port was deserted. Most of its population, forewarned, had departed, taking their valuables with them. But there was still the town of Gibraltar, a promising target along the coast from Maracaibo, and de l'Olonnais lost no time heading for it. He disembarked 380 pirates a short way down the coast from the town. The Spaniards had blocked the route, but the pirates fought their way through and entered Gibraltar in triumph. Every villager was taken prisoner. De l'Olonnais' reputation for savagery was obviously well known. He threatened that if they failed to hand over a ransom of 10,000 pieces of eight, their village would be burned to the ground. The terrified villagers paid up.

Sailing back up the coast, de l'Olonnais used the same method on the citizens of Maracaibo, who had returned once the pirates had gone. He achieved the same result, this time demanding a ransom of 30,000 pieces of eight. De l'Olonnais finally agreed to take 20,000 pieces and 500 head of cattle. In addition, the pirates ransacked churches for such treasure as bells, statues, and paintings, and emptied warehouses of provisions.

When de l'Olonnais and his crew arrived back in Tortuga, their welcome was enthusiastic. The expedition had brought each man 70 pieces of eight in cash and another 100 in silk and linen goods. This ensured a big turnout of hopefuls anxious to join de l'Olonnais' next expedition, and some 700 signed on with the now legendary "Brother of the Coast."

LAKE NICARAGUA

De l'Ollonais' destination was Lake Nicaragua, the largest lake in central America. With numerous towns and villages all along its rim, it promised rich plunder, but bad luck blighted the expedition all the way. De l'Olonnais reached the east coast of Nicaragua only to find that his ships were becalmed but drifting northward into the Gulf of Honduras. With both wind and current against them, the pirates were unable to regain their course and began to run short of supplies. They plundered the villages around the Gulf for food, such as maize, hogs, poultry, and turkeys, but it proved insufficient for their needs. Meanwhile, the Spaniards, alerted to the presence of the dreaded de l'Olonnais, set up a series of ambushes to prevent him reaching Puerto Cavallo. The pirates again fought their way through, but Puerto Cavallo was hardly worth the effort. It yielded little booty and in their frustration, the pirates burned it to the ground. By now, some of them had had enough and began to talk of returning to Tortuga. De l'Olonnais let them go and carried on with the rest, hoping to find better pickings in neighboring Honduras.

A particularly gruesome fate was reserved for De l'Olonnais. While still alive, he was hacked to pieces...the Indians threw "his body limb by limb into a fire and his ashes into the air."

DEATH IN BATTLE OR DEATH BY TORTURE
A death as gruesome as suffered by de l'Olonnais was not uncommon in the world of piracy. Pirates and privateers all sailed in the knowledge that such a fate could overtake them at almost any time if death in battle did not intervene first. Captain William Kidd was arguably one of the most famous of the Brethren of the Coast to fall foul of justice in the eighteenth century: he was hanged, and his body left to rot in a gibbet, as a warning to others.

But more bad luck plagued de l'Olonnais when his ship ran aground and refused to float off. De l'Olonnais decided to break up the ship and use its timbers to construct a longboat. Mindful of the pirate code and its democratic provisions, de l'Olonnais asked his men to vote on whether to accompany him to the River Nicaragua or remain in the Gulf of Honduras.

The pirates split up once again, and those voting for the river followed de l'Olonnais to its delta, only to be attacked by Spaniards and local Indians. Many pirates were killed. De l'Olonnais and the rest of the survivors fled back to their longboat. But after they reached the Gulf of Darien on the border between Panama and Colombia, the pirates were set upon by Indians, who made short work of them. A particularly gruesome fate was reserved for De l'Olonnais. While still alive, he was hacked to pieces and, according to Alexander Exquemelin, the Indians threw "his body limb by limb into a fire and his ashes into the air." This, Exquemelin concluded, "was the (fitting) end of a man who had spilled so much guiltless blood and committed so many grisly atrocities."

WILLIAM KIDD

William Kidd (1645–1701) was born in Scotland but went to the British colonies in America as a young man. Despite his youth, he scored speedy success as a trader and privateer and, by his twenties, was regarded as a member of the colonial elite. Later on, Kidd enhanced his reputation by proving his courage and leadership as the commander of a privateer vessel, the *Antigua*, during King William's War (1689–97), the first in a series of colonial conflicts between Britain and France. Kidd's prowess in engagements with French ships was noticed in high places, and in 1695, toward the end of the war, he received a Letter of Marque and Reprisal from the King of England, William III (1650–1702). Kidd's brief was to destroy pirates infesting coasts of the world and, for good measure, to continue his attacks on any French vessels he might encounter.

KIDD SETS SAIL FOR NEW YORK

The venture was financed by several English aristocrats, by King William and also by Kidd himself, although he had to sell the *Antigua* to raise the necessary funds. In

In 1699, when Captain Kidd was being hunted for piracy by the authorities, he buried some of his treasure on Gardiner's Island, New York. This included his Bible.

exchange, Kidd received a magnificent new vessel, a 313-ton (284-tonne) galley, the *Adventure*, which carried 34 guns and had a crew of 150 men—at least, in theory. Unfortunately, as he sailed the *Adventure* down the River Thames bound for his first destination, the coasts of Africa, he failed to observe the tradition of firing a salute as he passed by a Royal Navy yacht. This *faux pas* might have been forgiven as forgetfulness, but Kidd's crew committed an even worse solecism. Instead of making good the mistake, the crew showed their backsides after the yacht fired a shot to remind them of their duty. The captain of HMS *Duchess*, which was nearby, was so offended that he ordered most of Kidd's crew off the *Adventure* and, despite virulent protests, enlisted them in the Royal Navy then and there. Kidd was therefore forced to sail for New York with a minimum crew. There were enough of them to capture a French ship in mid-Atlantic, but not enough to deal with the forthcoming campaign against the pirates. Kidd therefore had to recruit more men in New York. Unfortunately, the New York recruits were a collection of rogues and criminals, many of them seasoned pirates. This was significant, for the privateering expedition became, in reality,

Captain Kidd was tried in London for piracy and the murder of one of his crew in 1698. Found guilty on all charges, he was executed at Execution Dock, London in 1701.

William Kidd's first venture into piracy. It was not a successful one. Kidd lost some 50 crewmen in a cholera epidemic in the Comoro Islands north of Madagascar. He failed to find pirates off Madagascar itself or at the southern end of the Red Sea, two of their most frequent haunts. He failed again when he attacked a convoy of ships belonging to the Mughal Emperor in northern India. Instead, the *Adventure* was beaten off by the convoy's escort, a British East India Company warship.

MURDER OF WILLIAM MOORE

But worst of all on this fated voyage, Kidd killed a member of the crew, his gunner William Moore. On October 30, 1697, a Dutch ship came in sight and Kidd refused Moore's suggestion that it should be attacked and plundered. Insults were exchanged. Kidd called Moore "a lousy dog," and in a fury threw an iron bucket at Moore, which felled him, fracturing his skull. He died the next day.

Moore's death appeared to be an accident, but it had very damaging consequences, leading to an outburst of charges against William Kidd. Men who had sailed under him suddenly recalled "atrocities," such as Kidd having ordered them to be hauled up by the arms and beaten with cutlasses or having made them watch as he tortured the crew of a trading vessel and afterward stole the cargo. In fact, the cargo was purloined by the crew themselves. When Kidd found out about the accusations, he demanded that his recalcitrant crew return the stolen goods, but the damage had been done. Kidd's probity became suspect and his "evil" deeds a certainty after the crew of the *Adventure* blackmailed him into an invidious position. On January 30 1698, Kidd seized a great prize, an Armenian vessel, the 441-ton (400-tonne) *Quedah,* which was sailing under the protection of the French crown. The ship contained an immensely valuable cargo of gold, silver, satins, muslins, and silks. Kidd commanded his crew to hand back this wondrous booty, but they refused. They maintained that the *Quedah* was fair game because it was protected by the French and therefore as good as French, and Kidd's instructions specifically allowed him to seize French ships.

William III, King of Great Britain. After he was sentenced to death, Kidd begged William to grant a reprieve, but to no avail. The king did not reply, and the sentence was duly carried out.

Captain Kidd's corpse was hung in chains by the River Thames until it rotted away. This was a customary practice and was meant to deter men from becoming pirates.

Kidd, who was already having problems controlling his crew even apart from the *Quedah* incident, had behind him an experience he did not want to relive on his current ship. The *Blessed William* had been taken from him by mutineers led by one Robert Culliford. Now, some eight years later, Kidd feared that there might be another Culliford among his current crew and realized that if he crossed them, this might easily provoke a mutiny. For this reason, Kidd gave in and kept the *Quedah,* which he renamed the *Adventure Prize*. But when the news reached England, it was interpreted in a much more insidious way. William Kidd, the British Admiralty decided, had become a pirate. Admiralty courts had once turned a blind eye to the excesses committed by privateers who slipped over legal limits, but not this time. As a result, Kidd became a target for Royal Navy captains, who were ordered to pursue and seize him, together with his accomplices "for the notorious piracies they had committed."

ROBERT CULLIFORD

Meanwhile, fresh trouble was brewing for the beleaguered Kidd. At the beginning of April 1698, he reached Madagascar, only to find that his nemesis from earlier days, Robert Culliford, was already in harbor at the Ile Sainte-Marie (St Mary's Island) in his frigate *Mocha*. Since 1690, Culliford had become an accomplished pirate with many prizes under his belt, and despite the seizure of the *Adventure Prize* and its splendid booty, Kidd's crew might well have viewed him as a better bet for their own prospects. In order to keep the peace, the privateer now forgave Culliford for the dirty trick he had pulled on him, but this did nothing to preserve the crew of the *Adventure Prize*. A large number deserted Kidd and signed on with Culliford. After this, Kidd was left with a loyal remnant numbering only 19 men. He returned to New York City in the *Adventure Prize*. On his arrival, Kidd learned that he had been labeled a pirate and a wanted man, with several British warships scouring the seas for him.

THE HANGING OF WILLIAM KIDD

The rope broke at the first attempt, and Kidd had to endure a second attempt, this one successful. The six associates tried with him were all pardoned just before his execution. Afterward, Kidd's corpse was 'gibbeted' (hung in an iron cage), and left to swing over the River Thames, where it could be seen by ships and crews passing by on their way out to sea, and taken as a warning against piracy.

The *Adventure Prize* was clearly a liability now, so Kidd hid it in the Caribbean and sailed back to New York in a sloop. On the way, he buried some of his treasure on Gardiner's Island, close to the eastern end of Long Island, New York. Kidd hoped to use the treasure as a bargaining counter when confronting the Earl of Bellomont, who had been appointed Governor of New York in 1695.

But things did not work out that way. On July 6, 1699, Bellomont ordered Kidd to be arrested, and afterward shipped him back to England, to be interrogated by Parliament. Kidd hoped that his friends and patrons would stand by him and get him off the hook. No such luck. Far from supporting him, his wealthy backers kept their distance and refused him the money and documents that could have formed the basis of a legal defense. Instead, Kidd stood trial at the High Court of Admiralty in London charged with five counts of piracy on the high seas and with the murder of William Moore in 1698. Incarcerated in the infamous Newgate Prison along with killers, cut-throats, thieves, and miscreants of every other kind, Kidd wrote letters to King William asking for reprieve. It did him no good. Kidd was found guilty on all charges and was hanged at Execution Dock in London on May 23, 1701.

As a result, Kidd became a target for Royal Navy captains, who were ordered to pursue and seize him, together with his accomplices, "for the notorious piracies he had committed."

BLACKBEARD

If any individual was a one-man warning against piracy, it was Edward Teach (1680–1715), who owed his nickname, Blackbeard, to the long, matted beard that covered his face from just below his dark flashing eyes and extended all the way down to his stomach. A tall, imposing presence, Blackbeard seems to have been more than half mad: he made his appearance as terrifying as possible by planting his beard with slow-burning matches, which were more normally used to fire guns and grenades. He thrust more lit matches into the brim of his cocked hat, slotted a cutlass into his wide leather belt, and wore three pairs of loaded pistols, cocked ready for firing, in a bandolier across his chest. The novelist Daniel Defoe called Blackbeard "a fury from Hell"—and so he appeared to his victims, one of whom was forced to eat his own ears, and to his crews, whom he regularly beat to enforce discipline and humiliated for his own perverse pleasure. Legend has it that he married 14 teenage girls at the same time and parked them on different Caribbean islands. According to Charles Johnson's *A General History of the Robberies and Murders of the Most Notorious Pirates,* the fourteenth wife was a 16-year-old and

> ... after he had lain all night, it was his custom to invite five or six of his brutal companions to come ashore, and he would force her to prostitute herself to them all, one after another, before his face.

Though stories like this one about Blackbeard abound, little seems to be known about his early life. Daniel Defoe records that he was born in Bristol, southwest England, and was baptized under the name of Edward Drummond. After serving on board a privateer in the War of the Spanish Succession, Blackbeard turned up in Nassau in around 1715 and joined a pirate crew captained by Benjamin Hornigold. Hornigold was impressed by Teach's boldness and great personal courage and put him in command of a sloop, one of a fleet of ships that was about to go a-pirating along the American coast.

Teach acquired his first substantial ship when the pirate fleet captured a large French ship: Hornigold was so pleased with Teach's performance that he gave him the vessel. Renaming it *Queen Anne's Revenge*, Teach fitted his ship with 40 guns, making her the most powerful and dangerous pirate vessel operating out of the Bahamas. The combination of the *Queen Anne's Revenge* and her formidable captain spread terror across the Caribbean after 1717, when Edward Teach set out on plundering raids of his own.

OUTGUNNING THE ROYAL NAVY

Early on, off the Caribbean island of St Vincent, Teach captured a magnificent prize, the English merchant ship the *Great Allen*. The *Great Allen*'s cargo was duly transferred to the holds of the *Queen Anne's Revenge*. After marooning the crew on St Vincent, Teach ordered their plundered ship to be set on fire and then sailed away, leaving them to survive if they could or, more likely, die.

When the news reached the Royal Navy base at Barbados, the *Scarborough,* a 30-gun frigate, was sent out to find Blackbeard. The *Queen Anne's Revenge* came in sight after a few days' sailing, but the pirate ship did not behave as expected. Normally, pirate ships chased by the Royal Navy either sailed off fast and escaped, or they struck their colors and surrendered. Not Blackbeard. He knew that the *Queen Anne's Revenge* could outgun the Royal Navy vessel, so he faced the oncoming *Scarborough* and battered her with heavy broadsides. The exchange of fire lasted several hours, but ultimately the *Scarborough* was so badly damaged that she had to retire and limp back to Barbados.

Within just a few weeks, Edward Teach had made his name and his reputation as a man to be feared, not only for the fighting power of his ship but for his personal ferocity. Tales were soon being told about his cruelty, which included his habit of shooting members of his own crew from time to time. This served a mad purpose for Blackbeard, who seemed to believed that shooting one or two crewmen now and then reminded the rest who he was.

But Blackbeard did not need to kill anyone to retain the upper hand on board his ships. The terror he inspired was quite enough to make his crews think twice before challenging him. The same was true for other pirate captains. Fear of Blackbeard was so pronounced that in May of 1717, when he encountered the American gentleman-pirate and one-time army major Stede Bonnet (1688–1718), he easily "persuaded" him to hand over his ship. One story about this encounter had it that Blackbeard burst out laughing when he saw the chubby-faced Bonnet, who was totally out of place among his rough-cut crew in his fine clothes and expensive periwig.

Nevertheless, this unlikely partnership was highly successful. Blackbeard the brute and Bonnet the novice went hunting together in the Caribbean, netting

Within just a few weeks, Edward Teach had made his name and his reputation as a man to be feared, not only for the fighting power of his ship but for his personal ferocity.

Lieutenant Robert Maynard of the Royal Navy (right) was the man who caught and finally killed the notorious Blackbeard (left).

In 1718, after navigating a difficult and dangerous route through the swamps around Ocracoke Island, a shallow-draft Royal Navy sloop commanded by Lieutenant Robert Maynard prepared to trap Blackbeard's ship, the *Adventure*.

several handsome prizes. They were still partners at the beginning of 1718, when they put in at Nassau to find bad news awaiting them: Woodes Rogers was on his way to Nassau as governor. Rogers' anti-pirate intentions were already known and when he heard the news, Teach departed Nassau with Bonnet almost straight away. They sailed northward to the town of Bath in North Carolina, where Teach knew he could rely on a suitably corrupt governor, his friend Charles Eden (1673–1722). Eden now granted him a "pardon," a piece of legal chicanery that allowed Blackbeard to use Bath as a pirate base to careen, refit, and resupply his ship before departing on new pirating ventures. In return, Governor Eden was to receive a share of the profits from the sale of Blackbeard's plunder, which was sold openly to the public and the merchants of Bath.

After a few weeks in North Carolina, Blackbeard and Bonnet headed south toward the Bay of Honduras, where they captured a sloop, the *Adventure* from Jamaica. As the sloop's new captain, Blackbeard appointed one of his officers, Israel Hands (whose name was borrowed by Robert Louis Stevenson for one of the pirates in his novel *Treasure Island*). Blackbeard's fleet of pirate ships was growing, with another sloop and several smaller vessels seized and added to it in the following eight weeks. It was time for the next big raid: in May of 1718, Blackbeard's fleet gathered outside the harbor at Charleston, in South Carolina, ready to implement an audacious act of piracy.

Blackbeard knew that inside Charleston harbor lay a dozen or more ships carrying valuable cargoes. Using his now substantial pirate fleet, he set up a blockade beyond the harbor, far enough away not to be easily seen, and waited for the ships to come out. A couple of days passed and then three large merchant ships emerged from the harbor entrance, to be quickly waylaid and captured. A few more days, and six smaller vessels fell into the same trap.

On boarding one of the larger ships, Blackbeard discovered that it held even richer cargo than he had imagined. Among the passengers was a member of the governor's council of South Carolina, Samuel Wragg, who was traveling with his small son. Wragg and his little boy were taken as hostages together with two other passengers. Blackbeard then demanded a ransom from the population of Charleston, not in cash or valuables, but in the form of medicine to treat the syphilis that was afflicting his crew.

Blackbeard sent several of his men to Charleston to underline the seriousness of this demand and impress on Governor Robert Johnson (1682–1735) and his council that if the "ransom" was not paid within two days, all four hostages would be killed and their decapitated heads piked and displayed in the town. But Blackbeard never did anything by halves. There was more to his threats than just these first demands. Non-compliance, he warned, would result in the destruction of the port of Charleston and the burning of every ship in the harbor.

There was little Governor Johnson could do but to give in and pay up. He sent a consignment of medical supplies worth around $594 (£300) and the hostages were duly released. But before they were set free, Blackbeard had all of them stripped down to their underwear and relieved of all their possessions. Samuel Wragg, the pirates discovered, had been carrying $119,000 (£60,000) and that became pirate booty, too. Afterward, the terrible Blackbeard, with Stede Bonnet still in tow, sailed for Topsail Inlet in North Carolina. Topsail Inlet, now known as Beaufort Inlet, lay close to Ocracoke Island, one of Blackbeard's favorite hiding places.

DOWNSIZING THE FLEET

Topsail was an ideal venue to rest and recuperate from recent exertions, and to careen, refit, and resupply his ships. Certainly, this seemed to be his intention. In the long term, however, he has other plans. After Charleston, Blackbeard realized that his large pirate fleet was not to his advantage. So many ships sailing together were too easily identified by pirate-hunters, and also complicated pirate operations. Most important of all, however, was the large number of pirates—320 of them—required to handle all these ships. The more numerous the crew, the more it cost to feed and equip them, and the less each of them, including Blackbeard, received as their share of the plunder. One really good vessel and a select crew were all that Blackbeard needed, and at Topsail Inlet he began to downsize his outfit.

The first to go was Stede Bonnet, who suspected nothing when Blackbeard

Stede Bonnet, a fairly wealthy landowner, suddenly turned pirate in 1717. Shortly afterward, Bonnet encountered Blackbeard, who at once recognized him as an amateur and took over his ship.

returned to him command of his ship *Revenge* and encouraged him to go back to Bath, in North Carolina to seek a "pardon" from Governor Eden. It did not occur to Bonnet that he was being "encouraged" with thinly veiled threats. He did as he was told and departed. Blackbeard was less subtle with his own men. When he started loading all the plunder captured by the pirate fleet onto his own sloop, the *Adventure,* some of them instantly smelled a rat and objected furiously. Their fury, however, was nothing compared to Blackbeard's. Exploding with rage, he marooned the objectors on a barren sandbar. Fortunately, Stede Bonnet came along later and rescued them, but Blackbeard's display of menace and wrath was quite enough to prevent other crewmen from making the same mistake. Most of them fled inland into North Carolina rather than risk remaining with their dangerous and volatile chief.

Once they had gone, only 40 pirates (one-eighth of the previous crew's strength) and one ship, the *Adventure*, remained with Blackbeard. The *Adventure* returned to North Carolina, where Blackbeard picked up another "pardon" from Governor Evans for his recent pirating activities, including the blockade of Charleston. Afterward, Blackbeard made for Ocracoke Island, where he met up with Charles Vane and enjoyed a week of drunken merrymaking before they parted company and Vane went off to resume pirating.

Blackbeard remained on Ocracoke for a while, trading with officials and merchants from North Carolina. But unknown to him as yet, a plot was brewing among the colony's planters to break his hold over Governor Eden and rid themselves of the pirate menace once and for all. To this end, they appealed for help to Governor Alexander Spotswood (1676–1740) of Virginia. They could not have made a better choice, for Spotswood's hatred of pirates amounted to an obsession. He gladly embraced the chance to hunt down and possibly destroy the diabolical pirate who had become the terror of the coastline from Honduras to Virginia and on to New York.

The heavy warships of the Royal Navy were unable to navigate the channels and sandbars surrounding Ocracoke Island, but shallow-draft sloops had no such trouble. Two sloops, one commanded by Lieutenant Robert Maynard, the other by a midshipman named Baker, and with crews totalling 60 men, set out on November 17, 1718. They successfully navigated their way to an inlet where Blackbeard's *Adventure* lay at anchor. By this time, Blackbeard had been forewarned of the expedition against him by Governor Eden's corrupt Collector of Taxes, Tobias Knight. However, perhaps because he was confident that the Royal Navy could not possibly navigate the treacherous waters around Ocracoke Island, Blackbeard appeared unconcerned. Little by little, the Royal Navy was able to draw closer, though the crew did have to

It took at least five more pistol shots and 20 strikes of the cutlass from Maynard's crew before he at last began to stagger, sway, and fall. By the time Blackbeard hit the deck, he was dead.

BLACKBEARD'S HEAD HANGS AT BATH
Lieutenant Maynard ordered one of his men to cut off Blackbeard's head and throw his corpse overboard. Subsequently, Maynard hung the head from the bowsprit of his ship, complete with its immense beard, still matted with the blood of battle. Later on, Blackbeard's head was stuck on a pike and went on public display in Bath, in North Carolina.

resort to throwing casks of water overboard to make their sloops sufficiently light to keep on floating.

THE LAW CLOSES IN

At last, Blackbeard understood the extent of the danger. He leapt into action and a running battle ensued with prolonged exchanges of small arms fire. Finally, Blackbeard roared out an invitation to Lieutenant Maynard to come aboard the *Adventure* and confront him in person. Maynard shouted back, promising Blackbeard no quarter. Then, suddenly, the *Adventure* moved off, possibly making for a channel that Blackbeard knew would enable him to reach the open sea and escape. He was thwarted by the wind and current in the inlet, however, and he now saw that the second Royal Navy sloop, commanded by Midshipman Baker, was approaching his ship. Blackbeard shot off a tremendous blast of gunfire, which killed Baker and most of his crew and badly holed their sloop.

The confrontation now proceeded in slow motion, for the wind dropped completely and Lieutenant Maynard's crew had to use their oars to catch up with the *Adventure*. The sloop was almost alongside Blackbeard's vessel when the pirate fired a vicious broadside, killing and injuring 21 of Maynard's crew of 35 men. The remaining 14 crew were up to the challenge, however. Following Maynard's orders to hunker down below the deck, they drew level with the *Adventure* to be greeted by a hail of grenades and bottles filled with gunpowder, shot and pieces of iron. Smoke swirled up over the scene of battle, obscuring the deck of the sloop. Peering through, Blackbeard saw the deck was empty and presumed that the crew of the sloop were either dead or incapacitated.

It was a fatal mistake. When Blackbeard and his men leapt over onto the sloop, the crew suddenly roared up from below decks, wielding cutlasses and firing a mass of shot. Lieutenant Maynard found himself confronting Blackbeard at point-blank range and at once, both of them fired their pistols. Blackbeard missed, but Maynard hit his target.

Blackbeard did not prove an easy kill. Although spitting blood, he remained on his feet and came at Maynard wielding his cutlass. Maynard prepared to fire a second time, but before he could do so, one of his crew slashed at Blackbeard, slitting his throat. Now, Maynard fired once more, hitting Blackbeard in the chest. Even this failed to finish him off. It took at least five more pistol shots and 20 strikes of the cutlass from Maynard's crew before he at last began to stagger, sway, and fall. By the time Blackbeard hit the deck, he was dead.

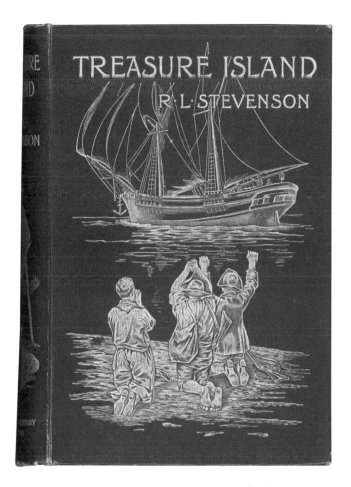

The cover of an edition of *Treasure Island* by Robert Louis Stevenson, the classic tale of pirates and buried treasure that is still popular today. The book was Stevenson's first big success as a novelist.

chapter 7

THE GOLDEN AGE OF PIRACY

Woodes Rogers was originally a Bristol merchant, one of several suffering big losses inflicted by pirates who were attacking their ships and seizing their cargoes. In 1708, a group of merchants clubbed together and fitted out a large ship, the 287-ton (260-tonne) *Duke*, with which they aimed to retrieve their losses. Woodes Rogers was chosen as commander, and William Dampier (1652–1715), the pirate and later Pacific explorer, as his navigator. They set out to harass the most likely source of rich prizes—the Spanish treasure fleets that plied the waters along the west coast of South America.

In an expedition that lasted three years, Rogers, now a privateer, captured two large Spanish treasure ships, carrying between them a fortune in bullion, precious stones, and Oriental silks. Reputedly, Rogers also rescued Alexander Selkirk (1676–1721) from Juan Fernandez island off the coast of Chile, where he had been marooned for four years. Selkirk was probably the model for the archetypal castaway Robinson Crusoe in the famous adventure story of the same name written by Daniel Defoe (1660–1731) and published in 1719–20.

In 1711, Rogers returned to Bristol in triumph, carrying captured cargoes worth around four million dollars, which was more than enough to compensate

The Duke, **built in England in 1708, was the flagship of the pirate-hunter Governor Woodes Rogers, who sailed into harbor at Nassau in the Bahama Islands in 1718.**

Alexander Selkirk, a Scottish buccaneer, quarreled with his pirate chief, William Dampier, and at his own request was marooned on Juan Fernandez Island in 1704. He was reputedly rescued by Woodes Rogers in 1709.

for the ships and cargoes lost by himself and his fellow merchants. Seven years later, once he had been installed as Governor of the Bahamas, Rogers soon got down to anti-pirate business. However, rather than wage war, he offered the pirates of Nassau, then known as New Providence, the King's pardon on the condition that they gave up piracy. It was a move that proved highly effective. Large numbers accepted the terms, driven perhaps by Rogers' reputation for severity. Only the big-time troublemakers, like Blackbeard (Edward Teach) or Charles Vane (c.1680–1720) were exempt. Blackbeard was killed in battle (*see* Chapter 6, Tales from the Caribbean) and Vane ended up on the gallows.

Piracy and privateering in the Caribbean were not entirely extinguished by these measures but, to the great relief of the inhabitants, attacks on the coasts and islands became much rarer occurrences. Letters of Marque and Reprisal, which had helped protect the Brethren of the Coast and other privateers, also became harder to come by. In addition, the Royal Navy saw to it that pirating in the Caribbean became much more difficult when the big prizes were kept out of reach by better security and more frequent patrols.

It was, however, unfortunate that the improvement proved to be only temporary as events in Europe created new opportunities and new venues for pirates to exploit. The catalyst that revived piracy some 30 years after Ratisbon (*see* Chapter 5, The Brethren of the Coast) was the Treaty of Utrecht, which brought to an end the 11-year War of the Spanish Succession. This opened the floodgates: thousands of seamen and soldiers, British (some of them privateers), Americans, Dutch, German, Danish, and French were released from military service and became unemployed. But they were not unemployable, for they had many years of training and experience behind them and were already hardened to seafaring, its routes, and its rough, often brutal, conditions. Coincidentally, the early eighteenth century saw a significant rise in trading and slaving across the Atlantic as traffic flourished between Britain, France, The Netherlands, Spain, and Portugal and their American colonies. The math was simple. Add a glut of manpower to a boom in trade and the answer is piracy, or more specifically, the Golden Age of Piracy.

NEW RECRUITS

Thus there was no shortage of new recruits, which included a fair number of sailors who lived in increasingly uncongenial conditions onboard slave ships. More applicants seeking fewer jobs created an employers' market, and shipmasters made the most of it by driving down both pay and the standards of accommodation, food, and other facilities until, finally, conditions for the sailors were almost worse than they were for the slaves they were helping to transport. Sailors, understandably, began to look for alternatives. It did not take them long to realize that piracy was a better bet, with its superior conditions, copious supplies of food, comradeship, promise of freedom and adventure, democracy as offered by the pirate code, and, above all, the chance to acquire a fortune.

In spite of these temptations and the large number of sailors who succumbed to them, the official slave trade remained buoyant, packing 500 slaves or more

But they were not unemployable, for they had many years of training and experience behind them and were already hardened to seafaring, its routes, and its rough, often brutal, conditions.

A TIME OF ABUNDANCE

The Golden Age is the name—some might say misnomer— given to the period up to around 1730, when there was a proliferation of pirates over an increased area of the world. A number of them departed the Caribbean to escape the hardline Treaty of Ratisbon; others preferred to continue pirating rather than accept the amnesty offered by Woodes Rogers. Instead, they removed to the coast of West Africa, with its hugely profitable trade in 'black gold' – the inhabitants of coastal areas, who were captured by hunters or bartered into slavery by their tribal leaders. 'Golden Age' pirates also sought wealth in the Indian Ocean, where fortunes were on offer to successful pirates who could seize priceless cargoes of silk, jewels, and ivory, and such spices as pepper, nutmeg, and cinnamon. A further hunting ground for Golden Age pirates lay in the British colonies in America.

The Treaty of Utrecht was signed in 1712 after the end of the War of the Spanish Succession. Afterward, thousands of well-trained sailors and navigators became unemployed. Many turned pirate.

Het tekenen vande VREDE tuſſchen Engeland Portug: Pruiſ. Savoje Holland en Vrankr: u Apr. 1713
la PAIX conclue entre l'Angleterre Portugal Pruſse Savoje Hollande et France l'u Avril 1713

into a ship in horrific, often fatal, conditions and transporting them across the Atlantic to the American and Caribbean colonies. It has been reckoned that in the early eighteenth century, some 25,000 slaves were shipped to the slave markets in the New World every year, making them valuable cargo for predatory pirates. Even more booty was on offer from the so-called "triangular trade." This developed between Europe, where the slaving ships originated; the African coast, where people were captured or exchanged with local rulers for cloth, beads, muskets, iron bars, or brandy; and, finally, the markets in the New World.

Once the slaves were sold, the ships that had delivered them to their servitude were loaded with sugar, cocoa, rum, and other exotic exports and sailed back to Europe, where the triangular trade began all over again. Needless to say, slave traffic passing both ways across the Atlantic was susceptible to pirate attack, as were ships carrying supplies for the colonists and afterward returning home with raw materials, precious metals, jewels, and other products of the New World.

When the Treaty of Utrecht helped to restart piracy, the greatest beneficiaries were the British. They enjoyed a head start over other combatants when the Treaty awarded them a license to supply slaves to the Spanish-American colonies, which, previously, had been strictly off-limits for foreigners. Even before the War ended in 1713, the British Royal Africa Company was already well established along the coast of Africa, whose coastline extended the 3045 miles (4900km) from Senegal in the north all the way south to Angola. Within this considerable stretch of shoreline, the Company controlled not only the slave trade but also the trade in gold, ivory, and other valuable commodities.

Of special interest to pirates was the series of forts constructed by the Company in order to guard these wondrously profitable centers.

A TREASURE HOUSE OF LOOT FOR THE TAKING

All this made the Guinea Coast a treasure house of loot, and pirates looking for prey had little difficulty in finding it. All they had to do was to sail down the coast of West Africa, locate the most profitable trading centers, and pick off the loot, virtually at will. This was the method employed, with impudent variations all his own, by one of the most successful operators in the Golden Age of Pirates. He was Howell Davis, the same Howell Davis who captured Bartholomew Roberts in 1719 and introduced him to piracy. Although Davis was not long on the scene—his career lasted for only 11 months in 1718–19 —he has long been considered one of the "greats" of the Golden Age.

He began pirating in the Caribbean, where he captured two French ships, one near Hispaniola, the other off Cuba. Davis appropriated their cargo, stores, and equipment. But his time in the Caribbean was cut short by the arrival of Woodes Rogers as Governor of Nassau, Davis being among those who refused the amnesty Rogers offered. Instead, he took his sloop, the *Buck*, across the Atlantic and started pirating along the west coast of Africa.

Onboard a pirate ship, a new recruit is shown being interviewed for a place among the crew. The more experienced he was, the better, for pirates needed to be consummate sailors and fighters.

Howell Davis had new and original ideas about how to obtain booty. Handsome and personable, he was a consummate con man who was able to persuade governors and their staff that he was an honest trader. He was also successful in another guise, as a Royal Navy officer with a disciplined crew, who were doubtless cleaned up for the occasion with all the necessary uniforms, weaponry, and flags to justify their false identities.

Davis's first port of call along the coast of West Africa was St Nicholas, one of the Cape Verde Islands. Here he charmed his way into the home of the Portuguese governor. Local traders were similarly taken in. Davis had no problems exchanging their wine and other products for goods onboard the *Buck,* which, in reality, were loot acquired from his French prizes seized in the Caribbean. Davis remained at St Nicholas for five weeks before moving on to another Cape Verde island, Maio, where he discovered several vessels with valuable cargo aboard berthed in the harbor. Davis and his crew thoroughly pillaged all these ships, apparently meeting no serious resistance to this blatant act of piracy. Before leaving Maio, Davis seized one of the vessels as his new flagship and renamed it *King James.* Embarking several new crewmen from the plundered ships, Davis

Slaves, newly captured along the coast of west Africa, had shackles placed on their ankles before being forced down into the hold of a slave ship. The dreaded Middle Passage across the Atlantic followed.

departed for his next destination, the Portuguese-ruled island of Santiago. Here, though, Davis met his match. Perhaps tales of his earlier deceptions had spread along the coast, for the governor of Santiago became very suspicious when the *King James* sailed into harbor looking for all the world like a friendly visitor. Davis, sensing the governor's hostility, attempted to surprise him with a night attack on the island's fort. The fort turned out to be empty, however, because the governor had withdrawn the garrison to his own residence, where another attack by Davis and his crew was met with a barrage of fire from muskets and pistols. Davis now made a hasty retreat, but not before tossing grenades into the governor's house and badly damaging his elegant and valuable furniture. For good measure, Davis and his pirates plundered the port of whatever goods and treasure they could find and, before they left, spiked the fort's guns. They then sailed away, heading for Gambia and the major trade base established there by the Royal Africa Company.

Once again, Davis had no trouble getting ashore. Hoodwinking his way into the governor's presence, Davis persuaded him to exchange the cargo aboard the *King James* for ivory and slaves. Davis even offered to throw in a few bottles of European liquor, which he claimed to have on board his ship. In fact, what Davis had onboard the *King James* was his crew, armed to the teeth and ready for his signal—a pistol shot out of the window—to storm the Company's fort. Suspecting nothing untoward, the governor invited Davis and two of his officers to stay for dinner. It seemed to be an enjoyable social occasion until Davis pulled out his pistol and told the shocked governor that he was now a prisoner. He then fired the prearranged pistol shot, alerting his crew to attack. Within a few hours, they had pillaged the fort of every treasure and valuable it possessed. The haul produced $3966 (£2000) in gold, an enormous amount at the time, along with substantial quantities of trade goods.

Howell Davis played the blameless trader twice more, once at Sierra Leone and once in the Gulf of Guinea where, from a Dutch merchantman, he claimed $29,745 (£15,000) in cash and a quantity of valuable cargo, his richest prize ever. Then, Davis went one trick too far. At his next port of call, the Portuguese island of Principe off the coast of present-day Gabon, he switched from his merchant identity to pose as an officer in the Royal Navy. But his mask of respectability slipped after a French vessel unexpectedly arrived in the harbor. Davis and his crew, unable to resist the temptation, thoroughly pillaged the Frenchman, transferring the loot to their own ship. The governor of Principe, now alerted to the true nature of his visitor, responded with a cunning trick of his own. Inviting Davis to his residence, he set a deadly trap—an ambush, in which Davis and all but one of his crewmen were killed. Feisty to the end, Howell Davis went on firing his pistols even after he lay mortally wounded on the ground. One of the legends to surround Howells had it that the pistols were still smoking in his hands when he died.

One of the legends to surround Howells had it that the pistols were still smoking in his hands when he died.

EDWARD ENGLAND

In the following year, the death occurred of another pirate, Edward England (*c.*1690–1720). Like Howell Davis, he left the Caribbean for Africa soon after the arrival of Woodes Rogers. England, whose real name was Edward Seager, was born in Ireland in around 1690, and was a stickler for the pirate code. However,

Edward England was a good deal more merciful than most other pirates when it came to treating prisoners. Unfortunately, his crew did not share his clemency and mutinied against him.

he added an unusual variation all his own. He showed that it was possible to be humane, if only by the standards of pirate brutality, by adding a modicum of mercy toward his opponents. England refused, for one thing, to use torture as a first resort when interrogating prisoners to make them yield important information, such as the whereabouts of hidden treasure. Instead, he preferred persuasion and cajolery and, if necessary, plied a prisoner with drink to loosen his tongue. This was hardly difficult, since most pirates and their captains were very heavy drinkers, imbibing mainly rum but pouring down their throats virtually anything else that was alcoholic. England himself was a keen tippler. He also recognized and appreciated valor in an opponent and responded by treating them more honorably than was the case with other, more sadistic, pirates.

PRIVATEER TURNED PIRATE

Edward England had served as a privateer during the War of the Spanish Succession. He was converted to piracy after a sloop, in which he was one of the mates, was captured by a certain Captain Christopher Winter while on its way from Jamaica to Nassau. It seems that Winter and his crew took a liking to England, who was more of a gentleman than most of their uncouth breed. Indeed, he commended himself so greatly that, after reaching Nassau, Winter took the extraordinary step of giving England a sloop of his own to command. The voyage from Jamaica to Nassau had not been long, but it was enough to convince England that the pirate life was for him.

From Nassau, he took his sloop out into the Caribbean on regular forays, and joined with other pirate captains in 1716, when they attacked a guardhouse on Cuba, which was keeping 350,000 pieces of eight in store. This splendid treasure represented the residue of millions of silver pieces dredged up from the seabed at a site in the Gulf of Florida, where a fleet of Spanish galleons had sunk in a storm. The Spaniards had done all the hard work, using diving equipment to fish up the sunken silver, and afterward transporting it to Havana. Typically, they tried to keep its existence secret but word got out and England and other pirate captains decided to remove it before it could follow the rest of the silver to the less easily assailable fort at Havana. They came to the guardhouse in force. In *A General History of Pyrates*, published in 1724, Daniel Defoe (1660–1731) reports that the pirates arrived in five ships and

came directly upon the place, bringing their little fleet to an anchor and, landing 300 men, they attack'd the guard, who immediately ran away, and thus they seized the treasure which they carried off, making…their way to Jamaica.

On the way, the pirates received a bonus: they captured a Spanish ship with another 60,000 pieces of eight onboard. Subsequently, Edward England was declared an outlaw for his part in this exploit. He made Nassau his headquarters until the arrival of Woodes Rogers forced him to leave and make for the coast of West Africa. One of the first prizes captured by England in his new hunting ground was a ship based in Bristol named the *Cadogan*. The *Cadogan*'s captain, a man named Skinner, was only too well known to England's crew. When they told their captain that this same Skinner had maltreated them, he set aside his

The Indian Ocean island of Mauritius was where Edward England and two pirates loyal to him were marooned. Although the island was inhabited, England chose to leave and return to Madagascar.

normal preference for mercy—not only for the sake of his men but for his own. Edward England knew enough about pirates and pirating to realize that if he failed to avenge the sufferings of his crew, he could easily face a mutiny or worse. Therefore England ordered Skinner to be tortured, then killed, as long overdue punishment.

Proceeding down the coast, Edward England and his crew captured a ship called the *Pearl*, exchanged it for his sloop and altered its name to the *Royal James*. England's next prizes were nine ships, three of which were plundered. Four others, probably unfit for pirate purpose, were burned, and the others were refitted as pirate vessels under the new names of *Queen Anne's Revenge* and the *Flying King*. Afterward, England exchanged the *King James* for a large Dutch ship, which was one of his next acquisitions, and renamed it the *Fancy*.

BATTLE AT JOHANNA

Next, having rounded the Cape of Good Hope, Edward England sailed into the Indian Ocean and arrived at the vast island of Madagascar off the southeast coast of Africa. On August 8, 1720, at Johanna, an island close to Madagascar, the *Fancy* and another of England's vessels sailed into the Bay, to be confronted by three trading ships belonging to the British East India Company. Recognizing the newcomers as pirates (England's ships were flying the black flag that indicated that no quarter would be given), the captains of two of the Company's vessels made a hasty escape. That left the *Cassandra*, under Captain James Macrae, to fight the pirates alone. Macrae decided to take them on, and a tremendous battle ensued. It lasted several hours and went on even after both the *Cassandra* and the *Fancy* ran aground.

At length, unable to save his ship from the pirates' gunfire, Captain Macrae and as many of his crew as survived, managed to escape and head for the shore. Meanwhile, the *Fancy* had been almost totally destroyed, and 90 of its crew had been killed. England had no intention of letting Macrae and his men get away. He went after them, but they managed to elude him for some days until, starving and desperate, they gave themselves up. England's brutal first mate John Taylor wanted to torture and kill Macrae in revenge for the pirates lost in the battle. But England saw that Macrae was a courageous man and refused to allow it.

Hours of argument followed, until England finally got his way and Taylor agreed to take the *Cassandra* as compensation. Macrae's ship was refloated and sailed to the small Indian Ocean island of Mauritius, 550 miles (885km) east of Madagascar. But Edward England was about to pay for his clemency. His crew were furious that

Edward Teach, known as Blackbeard, the most dreaded pirate of all. His behavior was terrifying enough, but he made himself an even more intimidating figure by wearing smoking fuses about his person.

their captain had allowed mercy to get in the way of what they considered their right to exact revenge on James Macrae. Like John Taylor, the pirates wanted blood for the losses they had suffered and the companions they had lost. Unfortunately for Edward England, the pirate code allowed for a captain deemed unsatisfactory by his crew to be replaced. The pirates accordingly removed England from his command and chose John Taylor in his place. Only two crewmen remained loyal to Edward England. One of them was described by Charles Johnson in *A General History of the Robberies and Murders of the Most Notorious Pyrates* (1724) as "a man with a terrible pair of whiskers and a wooden leg, being stuck round with pistols." (It is possible that this fearsome character was the model for Long John Silver in Robert Louis Stevenson's *Treasure Island*.)

England's brutal first mate John Taylor wanted to torture and kill Macrae in revenge. England saw that Macrae was a courageous man and refused to allow it.

155

England and his two companions were marooned together on Mauritius. Later, John Taylor claimed one of the greatest pirate treasure ever seized. Off the island of Bourbon near Madagascar, where the French had once tried to found a settlement, Taylor captured the Portuguese East Indiaman, the *Nostra Senhora do Cabo*. This prize of all prizes contained more than $1,628,600 (£800,000), enough to yield $8143 (£4000) for each of the 200-man crew, and 8400 small diamonds or, 42 per man.

Little wonder, then, that when John Taylor and his crew sailed back to the Cape Coast, they spent the next month or more partying and carousing. They also amused themselves by killing some of the local natives and setting fire to one of their villages. Later on, most of the pirates retired and some of them, together with John Taylor himself, received a pardon from the King of Spain

In the meantime, while his former crewmen were making themselves rich, Edward England and his two companions were not without resources. They managed to make a small craft out of scraps of wood and sailed it back to Madagascar, were they came ashore at St Augustine's Bay in the south of the island. But this was the last effort Edward England was able to make. Reportedly, he survived for a time by begging food from the natives of Madagascar. Either he starved or he fell foul of one of the many fevers that proliferated on the island, but he died shortly after arriving back on Madagascar, the most merciful of pirates and, in the end, a victim of his own generosity. Surprisingly enough, considering how close to death he had come, James Macrae survived and later returned home a hero to his native town of Greenock, in Scotland.

CHARLES VANE

Other pirates of the Golden Age preferred to remain closer to home than either Howell Davis or Edward England. Once Woodes Rogers had made the Caribbean too hot for them, they shifted north a latitude or two to prey on the coasts of North America, where the prizes were just as profitable. One of these pirates was Charles Vane (*c*.1680–1720), who began his career in 1716 as a member of a pirate crew led by Henry Jennings (died 1745). Jennings specialized in attacking and plundering the camps set up by the Spaniards to handle booty salvaged from galleons that had sunk in storms or other foul weather off the eastern coast of Florida. This form of piracy meant easy pickings. The Spanish salvagers brought the proceeds ashore, and Jennings and his crew stole them. But this joyride came to an end after the arrival of Woodes Rogers in 1718. Henry Jennings accepted the King's Pardon offered by Rogers, but Charles Vane refused to follow suit. More than that, Vane did not emulate other pirates, like Howell Davis and Edward England, who left the Caribbean to go a-pirating elsewhere. Instead, Vane went on capturing and plundering ships in or near the Caribbean Sea and gave notice of his defiance of Rogers and his mission by attempting to prevent the new governor from landing at Nassau.

Rogers sailed in with five vessels, including his flagship, the 507-ton (460-tonne) East Indiaman *Delicia*, a guard of two warships, the *Rose* and the *Milford*, and two sloops, *Buck* and *Shark*. Rogers, who was well aware of Charles Vane's intransigence, blocked the harbor at Nassau and, at nightfall, dispatched *Buck* and *Shark* to apprehend Vane and his six-gun sloop, the *Ranger*. But Vane was ahead of him. Guessing Rogers' intentions, he filled one of his recent prizes,

Either he starved or fell foul of one of the many fevers that proliferated on the island, but he died shortly after arriving back on Madagascar, the most merciful of pirates and, in the end, a victim of his own generosity.

Calico Jack Rackham wore bright calico clothes— hence his nickname. Rackham was moderately successful, but was executed in 1720 at Port Royal, Jamaica. His body was hung in a cage to deter others from piracy.

a French vessel, with explosives and set her on fire. Fireships had long been a common form of attack at sea and the one most dreaded by sailors. A vessel made of wood was only too vulnerable: once the flames had spread to the target ship, there was little chance of escape. Jumping into the water was hardly a strategy for survival.

Fortunately, Rogers' small fleet managed to evade disaster, by breaking up the blockade at the entrance to Nassau harbor and sailing out into the open sea beyond. Charles Vane waited until daylight, then ran up his black pirate's flag and moved out of the harbor, firing a few shots as he went as a gesture of impudence. He then disappeared into the vast expanse of the Atlantic Ocean.

But Woodes Rogers was not a man to give up easily. Once he was safely ashore at Nassau, he made a second attempt to capture Vane. Rogers sent a former pirate, Captain Benjamin Hornigold (died *c.*1719), to chase down the recalcitrant pirate and any others he could find. Hornigold captured several of them, but not Charles Vane. The vessels forced out of the harbor by the pirate were still close by, but they were unable to catch him and Vane evaded them once more. Once he was safely away, Vane sent word to Woodes Rogers, vowing to return to Nassau and burn his flagship, the *Delicia*.

REVELLING, PARTYING, FEASTING, AND CAROUSING

Meanwhile, Charles Vane made for the American coast, attacking and plundering cargo ships as far away as Long Island, New York. In September 1718, after three months a-pirating, Vane met up with the notorious Edward Teach at Ocracoke island, off Cape Hatteras, a promontory in North Carolina. Teach and Vane had known each other for two or three years, ever since Vane had turned pirate. Both of them now took advantage of the natural terrain Hatteras, which offered an almost impenetrable hiding place for pirates. No one unfamiliar with the inlets and shallows of the Cape, which was fringed by trees tall enough to conceal the masts of ships, would have been able to find a safe way through the elaborate criss-cross of channels, with their dangerous currents and ever-shifting sandbars. But Blackbeard and Vane were well acquainted with the secrets of the Cape and

Pirate flags were always fearsome. The so-called Jolly Roger "skull and crossbones" flag was the most familiar. On this flag, hoisted aloft by Calico Jack Rackham, the crossbones were replaced by crossed cutlasses.

had no difficulty reaching a safe anchorage. Together with their crews, they spent a riotous week revelling, partying, feasting, and carousing in one of the biggest pirate gatherings ever held. Drink flowed freely. And there was plenty of sex on offer, as the pirates were serviced by female prisoners and whores from the mainland. Vane's crew provided fiddlers while Blackbeard brought other musicians to Ocracoke Island to provide the music for dancing. So secure did Vane and Blackbeard consider this venue to be that neither was bothered about betraying their presence to the authorities. The pirate crew were allowed to celebrate around huge bonfires that flamed and roared on the beach, lighting up the sky.

Once it was all over, Vane and Blackbeard parted company. Blackbeard remained at Ocracoke, conducting business with merchants from the mainland. Charles Vane sailed away to resume cruising along the American coast, locating and plundering several ships. Then, one day early in 1720, Vane made a big mistake. As his ship was moving through the so-called Windward Passage between Cuba and Hispaniola, a large, slow-moving merchantman flying the French flag came into view. The Frenchman appeared to be a splendid prize and Vane moved in to take advantage. He gave chase, only to discover as he neared the ship that it was not a merchant vessel after all but a man-o'-war in disguise, powerfully armed with heavy guns. The warship let loose a mighty salvo and Vane, realizing that he was totally outclassed, opted to make a run for it. The man-o'-war chased after him but Vane's sloop, the *Ranger* was a fast mover and managed to get away. Vane had always avoided an unequal fight on the premise that it was better to live to fight another day than to risk destruction. Vane's crew, however, disagreed. For them, discretion was not the better part of valor: it was cowardice.

While the chase was still on, a majority of the crew, led by Vane's quartermaster Calico Jack Rackam (1682–1720), urged him to take on the Frenchman and fight it out, whatever the outcome. Vane refused. The French man-o'-war had more guns and was twice the size of the pirate ship. The pirates, he argued, would be destroyed and their ship sunk before they could get close enough to board her. Although pirates had the right to depose a captain for cowardice or any other misdemeanor, this did not apply while combat was going on. Vane therefore won the argument while the chase was continuing, but afterward, Calico Jack and the pirates lost no time invoking their right to replace an unsatisfactory captain.

Vane had never possessed the makings of a popular leader. He was too arrogant to commend himself to his crew. If anything, he treated them with contempt and also had a much-feared reputation for mindless cruelty. He would often torture and murder the prisoners he took on the ships he captured. Worse than that, as far as his crew were concerned, he frequently broke the provisions of the pirate code and cheated them of their fair share of booty. Charles Vane, therefore, did not have much going for him when his crew accused him of running scared and voted him out of office. Calico Jack became the new captain. Vane and the 15 pirates who remained loyal to him were placed in an open boat, with food, water, and weapons. They were set adrift and Calico Jack sailed away. Vane headed south into the Caribbean, heading for Jamaica and was just off the northwest coast of the island when he and his minimal crew managed to capture

Vane had always avoided an unequal fight on the premise that it was better to live to fight another day than to risk destruction.

three small craft, probably fishing boats. Vane and his companion pillaged these boats and persuaded some of their crewmen to join him.

Those who declined the invitation sailed off in two of the fishing boats while Vane kept the last one and sailed on toward the Gulf of Honduras. Vane accomplished some small-scale pirating in the Gulf, though none of the prizes he captured was of much worth. Then came disaster. In March 1719, both of Vane's craft were wrecked in a fierce storm that drowned most of his crew. Vane himself managed to reach a small uninhabited island, where he survived by begging food from natives who visited the island to catch fish and turtles.

CONDEMNED TO HANG

Charles Vane, it appeared, was saved at last, but bad luck deemed otherwise. The rescue ship encountered another vessel at sea and its captain was invited onboard. Vane was aghast when he saw that the captain was none other than Charles Holford. He tried to hide among the rest of the crewmen, but Holford spotted him and revealed his identity. Vane protested vigorously, but it was no use. He was put in irons and Holford took him to Jamaica, where he handed him over to the authorities. Vane was duly tried and found guilty of piracy. On March 29 1720, he was hanged at Gallows Point, Port Royal.

"By God!" Sympson cried, "I have lain with that bitch three times, and now she comes to see me hanged." The crowd, it seems, was amused.

After a few weeks, a ship from Jamaica captained by Charles Holford an ex-pirate friend of Vane's arrived at the island. Vane, who was by this time desperate, implored Holford to take him onboard. Holford refused, fearing that in no time at all, Vane would organize a mutiny and steal both his ship and his crew. The next ship to visit the island arrived a few days later, but Vane had learned a lesson from his encounter with Holford. He gave a false name and pretended to be an unfortunate shipwrecked sailor, vowing to prove his honesty and usefulness if only the ship's captain would rescue him. The ruse worked. The captain of the second ship neither knew who Charles Vane was nor what he looked like and took him off the island.

The defiance of men like Charles Vane gave a dramatic flourish to their bid to continue operating in the Caribbean in spite of Woodes Rogers. But it was a final flourish, for by the 1720s pirates were again facing the only force that had succeeded in crushing piracy in all the thousands of years it had lasted: seafaring nations with the power to intervene and the will to make that intervention tell.

THE FIGHT AGAINST PIRACY

Even though success had often proved temporary in the past, new punitive deterrents were about to be applied that made the campaign against piracy more formidable than ever before. Among them was the example set by the penalties imposed on the survivors of Bartholomew Robert's crew, who fought alongside their captain in his last great battle of 1722. The message was that pirates could no longer hope to receive pardons or rely on the collusion of corrupt officials or the bribes that had been handed out in exchange for better behavior.

Appeasement was now at an end. In its place was retribution. Of the 95 crewmen formerly led by Bartholomew Roberts—the "House of Lords," as they called themselves—21 served prison terms of varying lengths in England. Another 20 were sentenced to seven years' hard labor in the mines of the Royal Africa Company. This was a death sentence deferred, for none of the prisoners survived to be released. Another 54 were condemned to hang. The oldest among them was 45 years of age; the youngest was 19. Their executions were long, drawn-out affairs, possibly deliberately, in order to demonstrate what happened to pirates under the new, more retributive rules. Starting around April 4 1722, small groups of condemned pirates were taken from their dungeons beneath Cape Coast Castle in southern Africa, with their hands tied behind their backs, and accompanied to the scaffold by a guard of Royal Africa Company soldiers.

At the scaffold, a crowd of Company employees, sailors, slavers, and sensation seekers (who were never far away on such occasions) waited to see the men die. The pirates showed no remorse; one of them, "Lord" Sympson, even

Panoramic view of Port Royal, Jamaica. A thriving center of trade in the seventeenth century, Port Royal was known as the "richest and wickedest city in the world." It was popular with pirates and privateers.

161

An executed pirate hung high up in a cage. This was a common sight by the River Thames in London or at Port Royal, Jamaica. The dead pirates hung in their cages until they rotted.

joked with the crowd when he spotted a woman who had been a passenger onboard one of the ships seized by Bartholomew Roberts. "By God!" he cried, "I have lain with that bitch three times, and now she comes to see me hanged." The crowd, it seems, was amused.

The hangings ended after 16 days, on April 20, when the last batch of 14 prisoners was executed. A special fate awaited the 18 most reprehensible members of the "House of Lords." Their corpses were dipped in tar to preserve them, and then hung in chains from gibbets until they rotted away. The gibbets were placed where the crews of all ships approaching the Cape Coast could see them, as a warning.

Such a warning was not confined to the Cape Coast or even to the crews who visited it. It was meant to go out to all pirates everywhere and had special significance on Madagascar, which had a great deal to lose from the coming campaign to eliminate piracy. Madagascar lies at a distance of 250 miles (400km) from the east coast of Africa, across the Mozambique Channel, and is the world's fourth-largest island. With an area of some 228 square miles (592 square km), it is extensive enough to accommodate its own range of mountains, measuring up to 9515ft (2900m) high. Along its eastern side are copious forests and a mass of rivers, which are fed by an annual downpour.

HEAVEN ON MADAGASCAR

By the middle of the seventeenth century, Madagascar had become what might be called the Tortuga of the east, though on a very much larger scale. It was frequently visited by European traders—and pirates. For all of them, whether legal or illegal, Madagascar was an ideal base to re-equip, revictual, repair, and careen their ships. For the pirates, the island offered plenty of secluded coves, sheltered harbors and other hiding places where their ships would be difficult to find—if, that is, there was anyone daring enough, or foolhardy enough, to look for them.

There were other advantages, too. The weather on Madagascar was generally pleasant. Food, fresh water, and liquor were plentiful. So were local women. The pirates found that the island was perfectly placed for plundering purposes. Trading ships stopping off at Madagascar were easy victims of theft and pillage. Slave ships, too, called at Madagascar, carrying some of the most valuable cargoes of all. The nearby Red Sea also provided rich pickings. So did the shipping that sailed past the island on the way back from the Oriental markets, with such exotic goods onboard as silks, brocades, spices, ivory, or precious metals and jewels. As a pirate haven, therefore, Madagascar was hard to beat and it possessed two further unique advantages. In the seventeenth and eighteenth centuries, unlike the Caribbean, the coast of East Africa had no European settlements that needed to be governed by busybody officials like Woodes Rogers. Above all, Madagascar belonged to no one. The French had once attempted to claim the whole island, but lacked the power to make good their claim. No formal, island-wide government existed, nor did any universally accepted set of laws on Madagascar, except for those the pirates made for themselves. There was nothing to prevent pirates from becoming rich men, able to retire and live out their retirement in luxury. Some pirates considered Madagascar so congenial that they settled there. From time to time, 40 or 50 of them would found small settlements, where they lived with their wives and children. Occasionally, a pirate chieftain might proclaim himself "king" of his patch of territory; with no rivals to dislodge him, he could reign over his "realm" for many years. One of them was John Rivers, who created his "kingdom" in 1686 and ruled it for more than 30 years, until his death in 1719.

IMPERIAL NATIONS CRUSH THE "SWEET TRADE"

The "sweet trade," the euphemism for piracy coined by the pirates themselves, remained sweet for some 30 years after Madagascar reached its peak of prosperity in around 1690. But the new, more intensive anti-piracy campaigns turned the trade sour, as the imperial nations of Europe—Britain, France, The Netherlands, Spain, and Portugal—found that the need to protect colonial trade became more urgent as trade increased. The anti-pirate campaigns took several forms, the first

AS AT SEA, SO ON LAND
The pirate laws of Madagascar were basically the same as the Articles of Agreement, Pirate Code, Custom of the Coast—however it was called—simply transferred from ship to shore. All pirate ships and crews operating in or out of Madagascar were tied to a common code, which laid down the rights and obligations of everyone on board ship, from the lowliest apprentice right up to the captain. The loyalty and tolerance created was remarkable considering the volatile ferocity that characterized so many pirates. For instance, crews comprising several nationalities, who might otherwise be naturally opposed to each other—including Scots, Swiss, English, Dutch, American, and runaway black slaves – set out on expeditions together and obeyed the laws of the code without undue friction.

of them economic. In 1698, the pirates based in Madagascar found their income crippled when their main supplier and dealer in New York, Frederick Philipse, was forced out of business by the British governor of New York, Richard Coote, Earl of Bellomont (1636–1701). Bellomont used the simple expedient of seizing Philipse's ships and confiscating them, together with their cargoes. All these cargoes were of immense value, for they were stuffed with loot stolen by the Madagascar pirates. With this, the American market for illicit goods was severed. Another governor in the American colonies, Francis Nicholson of Virginia (1655–1727), chased a gang of pirates over the border into Pennsylvania, where he captured them. For good measure, Lord Bellomont saw to it that Pennsylvania's corrupt acting governor, William Markham (1635–1704), who had been protecting the pirates, was removed from his job.

Nicholson himself went to war and personally directed one battle off the coast of Virginia between a pirate ship and a coast guard vessel. During the fighting, he used a cunning incentive to encourage his crew. According to an eyewitness, the valiant governor

Vasco da Gama, last of the Portuguese navigators who pioneered the sea route from Europe to Asia over a period of 80 years, voyaging further and further along the African coast. Da Gama reached India in 1498.

never stirred off the quarterdeck, but by his example, conduct and plenty of gold which he gave amongst the men, made them fight bravely, till they had taken the pirates' ship with a hundred and odd prisoners, the rest being killed.

THE ROYAL NAVY GROWS IN MIGHT

Eventually, the economic pressure, the direct action against the pirates, and the retributive laws exacted their toll. So did the increasing prominence and power of the Royal Navy, which transformed itself from a small, defensive force into a highly professional service— the world's largest—and one that was constantly on patrol, watching out for illegal activity. It was now much more dangerous for pirates to prowl the seas and oceans seeking and attacking prey, and far less likely that they would get away with it. The loss of Madagascar and

TRIAL AND EXECUTION ON SITE
The British government added to the onslaught by introducing new laws
that made it easier to prosecute the pirates. One of these laws did away
with the practice of returning captured pirates to England for trial. Instead,
they were tried and executed wherever they were apprehended. It was a
policy that taught the locals a stern lesson, sped prosecutions, and saved
money, much to the pleasure of miserly eighteenth-century governments.

the Caribbean, with their invaluable facilities, was also a crucial factor in
bringing down the edifice of piracy as the world had long known it. Many pirates
decided to call it a day. Some individuals remained defiant and carried on as
best they could, but now they were more of a nuisance than a danger; not quite
powerless, but not far from it either.

After around 1730, no pirate of the stature of the Brethren of the Coast or
their successors in the Golden Age of Piracy challenged the major maritime
nations. By that time, pirates had only two choices: give up and retire, or carry
on and risk capture and death. Either way, they had to face the same sobering
truth. The days of adventure and freedom, of democratic rights granted by the
pirate code, of fabulous wealth brought by the "sweet trade"—those days were
well and truly over.

Madagascar, the world's
fourth-largest island, was
a haven for pirates and
privateers in the
eighteenth century. The
island's harbors were also
used for legitimate
commerce, and ships
were sometimes
plundered in port.

chapter 8

PIRACY TODAY

Piracy on the high seas has been a feature throughout the centuries. After 1914, however, pirate attacks became increasingly rare as the British, French, Dutch, and others patrolled trade routes to protect their overseas empires. The introduction of steam power at the end of the nineteenth century made navies more efficient because ships, unlike their predecessors in the age of sail, were no longer subject to the vagaries of the weather or the storms at sea. But technological advances did not bring the story to an end. In whatever age, the poor and the desperate are always ready to turn pirate to earn an income or even just to stay alive.

In the twentieth century, China was a case in point. In a country where the vast majority of inhabitants could do little more then scratch a living that left them teetering on the edge of survival, pirates had long been active—and successful—and they remained a stern challenge to governments and a scourge to shipping. In August 1911, pirates fought a ferocious battle with government gunboats near Canton (now Kwangchow) on the Pearl River. The gunboats were equipped with guns and muskets, while the pirates used three traditional junks powered by sails and oars. The unequal struggle soon resolved itself. One of the junks blasted by gunfire carried almost six months' booty, which was salvaged afterward. The gunboat crews saved around 25 pirates, who had been flung into the river when their vessel sank.

An anti-piracy patrol monitors the shipping on waterways prone to piracy. The ships are stuffed with modern equipment for detecting, locating, and following pirates.

167

Government officials spent three days searching the villages along the Pearl River, as well as the villagers' junks, and captured 50 prisoners to take back to Canton. Several of the prisoners were identified as Colowan pirates and were duly executed.

Colowan Island was part of the Portuguese enclave of Macau at the mouth of the Pearl River. Macau had been leased to Portugal in 1557 and had long been a haunt of pirates. The settlement there was a constant irritant to the Portuguese, who were additionally embroiled in a dispute with China over their territorial rights in Macau. In the middle of July in 1910, just over a year before the gunfight on the Pearl River, Colowan pirates had captured a party of Chinese students, doubtless with a view to extracting ransoms. The Governor of Macau, however, decided on military action and sent troops to rescue the students. This gave the Chinese a chance to strike at the Portuguese by sending their own soldiers to back up the Colowan pirates. Nor was this a primitive force. The Chinese were equipped with modern weapons and used smokeless powder, which allowed the use of semi- and fully automatic firearms.

MORE POWERFUL WEAPONS

World War I, which began not long after these outbreaks of piracy in China, provided a major boost to modern technology. By the end of the war in 1918, weapons were many times more powerful—and lethal—than they had been at the beginning, just four years earlier, and their effectiveness increased even further in the years leading up to and during World War II. Naturally enough, wartime conditions made the seas more dangerous for all seafarers, including pirates. Especially during World War II, weapons evolved in both form and power to a degree never previously achieved. By the time hostilities ceased in 1945, there was a vast amount of sophisticated armament left over from the fighting. At the same time, navies began downsizing and shedding surplus weaponry, which eventually made its appearance on the black market. From there, of course, a large amount of it found its way into the wrong hands.

This made it easy for criminals of all kinds, including would-be pirates, to get their hands on a range of armor never available before on the open market, such as rifles, automatic machine-guns, grenades, bazooka rocket launchers, flame-throwers, gunboats, and a great deal of the other paraphernalia that made modern warfare so horrifically destructive. Subsequently, many twentieth-century pirates

…navies began downsizing and shedding surplus weaponry, which eventually made its appearance on the black market. From there, of course, a large amount of it found its way into the wrong hands.

COLOWAN ISLAND
Around 2000 troops were involved in the fighting on Colowan Island. The Chinese suffered numerous casualties, and the Portuguese one corporal killed and dozens wounded. Later, the Portuguese emphasized the lesson they sought to teach both the pirates and the Chinese forces. They sent a gunboat to bombard the pirate settlement on Colowan, destroying several houses and killing many of the islanders. The captive students were ultimately rescued, but the dispute over the ownership of Colowan was never properly resolved. The issue became redundant with the handover of Macau to the People's Republic of China in 1999.

This illustration, reprinted from the German magazine *Das Neue* published in 1918, shows Chinese pirates armed with daggers engaged in boarding a ship after sailing close to it and throwing a line onboard.

acquired pretty well every technological advance that suited their purposes. From the 1980s, and on into the twenty-first century, equipment became increasingly sophisticated, which suited their purposes admirably. Where pirates of the past acquired their loot by means of cutlasses, muskets, and cannon, their modern counterparts have at their disposal computers, hand-held global positioning systems, phones linked to satellites, high-power telescopes, radar tracking systems, a wide range of automatic weapons, and a network of brokers willing and able to buy and sell their stolen goods.

BOYSIE SINGH

But no matter how high-tech equipment becomes, the old ethos survives, and the search for adventure and the quest for personal freedom continue to be major motivations for going a-pirating. In the 1950s, the Caribbean pirate Boysie Singh, alias Julius Mama (1908–57) was in many ways the heir to the legendary swashbucklers of the seventeenth and eighteenth centuries. Like Bartholomew Roberts or Blackbeard, Boysie Singh was a bit of a dandy and liked to appear in brightly colored zoot suits and ten-gallon hats, wearing numerous rings on his

On March 18 2006, the USS guided missile cruiser *Cape St. George* was attacked by pirates, who did not have things all their own way. The picture shows a pile of weapons confiscated from the raiders.

fingers. He was also a celebrity and an old-style "Mr. Big," who could impose his personality and his will on others in order to enforce their obedience. But Boysie Singh parted company with some of his pirate predecessors in one very important way. Unlike Roberts, John Phillips, or the Brethren of the Coast, he never allowed himself to be limited in what he could and could not do by any code of conduct. For him, there was no such thing as honor among thieves.

Boysie Singh was born on April 5, 1908 at Woodbrooke, Port of Spain, on the island of Trinidad. He was only a part-time pirate, but after 1947 his other criminal activities quickly made him the most feared villain at large in the Caribbean. He was a mass murderer, arsonist, gangster, and gambler with his own string of night clubs. As pirates, Boysie and his gang used to board fishing vessels, kill the crew, remove the engine for sale in Venezuela, and sink the boat. Before leaving the scene, the pirates made sure that no stray evidence of their crime, such as a floating spar or piece of clothing, was left behind. For nine years after World War II until 1956, he and his men spread terror along the waters that lay between Trinidad and Venezuela on the coast of South America, which had for years been infested by drug smugglers.

Boysie Singh inspired a dread that was shared by most of the population of Trinidad, who had no doubt of his evil temperament and capacity for killing. At one time, he was thought to have committed more murders than anyone else in the world. In fact, he became the "bogeyman" of Trinidad. Mothers would frighten their children by saying, "Behave yourself or Boysie's going to get you!"

Boysie's career in crime came to an end after the disappearance of a number of Trinidadian fishermen, together with their boats. Some estimates put the number of missing men as high as 400. First suspicions were aroused in 1950, when two fishermen left Port of Spain in a pirogue, a long, narrow canoe made from a single tree trunk. The pirogue was powered by an outboard engine. Conditions were favorable that day. It was calm and the sea was unruffled. The two crewmen, both experienced sailors, vanished and never returned to Trinidad. Shortly afterward, two more men set out to sea and were last seen at around 10.00 p.m., hove to beside a larger craft. They never came back, either.

Fishermen on Trinidad were becoming afraid to venture out to sea when the mystery deepened still further. The body of Philbert Peyson, one of Boysie's men who specialized in burglary, hold-ups, and piracy, was washed up on the shores of a bay near the Trinidad Yacht Club. Peyson's corpse was tied to a slab of rock weighing some 97lb (44kg). It was strongly suspected that Peyson had been killed by Boysie and his gang for betraying them to the Trinidadian authorities.

A while before this grisly revelation, Boysie Singh had extended his activities to fishing. The police on Trinidad, always aware of the dangerous criminal in their midst, began to take an extra interest in him. Plenty of evidence soon turned up for the police to sift. For example, a cloth merchant from Venezuela complained that three of his relatives had disappeared after they put out to sea from Port of Spain carrying cargo worth $3000 (£1525). Neither they nor their cargo reached Venezuela. Subsequently, the police raided the home of Boysie's wife and 20-year-old son Anthony, where they found silk and tweed materials that matched those carried by the missing men. They also discovered an outboard motor and equipment from the first of the vanished fishing vessels. A few days later, the owner of one of the missing boats saw Anthony Singh

Boysie Singh inspired a dread that was shared by most of the population of Trinidad, who had no doubt of his evil temperament and capacity for killing.

attempting to hold up the truck containing his day's catch of fish. When another truck approached, Anthony hurriedly drove off, but he was later arrested and charged with attempted robbery, then freed on bail.

Boysie, meanwhile, was in jail with three members of his gang, accused of murdering Philbert Peyson. This was the second time that Boysie had been charged with murder, and it was also the second time that he escaped the death penalty. But justice soon caught up with him. It was, third time unlucky for Boysie Singh in 1957, when he was put on trial in Port of Spain for the murder of his niece, Thelma Haynes, and hanged. By the time Boysie was executed, the world was moving on fast, both socially and technologically, in ways that enabled piracy to revive and gave it new clothes to wear.

INCREASE IN WORLD TRAVEL

By the late 1950s, the devastation inflicted on Europe by World War II had largely been repaired. Now, for the first time, there was a growing market for world travel—and a new source of potential booty. These years were marked by the development of aircraft, in particular the so-called jumbo jets introduced by the American Boeing corporation in 1970. The first of these giant jet aircraft, the Boeing 747, could carry up to 550 passengers. From the pirates' point of view, this meant more passengers on more aircraft, physically isolated from the outside world with no easy chance of escape when the pirates came to call. In addition, the years after World War II brought a significant increase in the number of cargo ships, freighters, and oil tankers plying the high seas, offering yet more possibilities for plunder. Not that smaller vessels were immune to the attentions of the new pirates of the twentieth and twenty-first centuries. Even small vessels—yachts, private boats, fishing smacks—were in the frame for pirate attacks. In the summer of 1997, for example, a British couple on holiday in Greece were sailing around the island of Corfu in their hired yacht, when masked men came onboard and threatened them with grenades and assault rifles. The couple were stripped of their possessions and the boat's navigation equipment was stolen. Ultimately, the pair were rescued by the Greek coast guard, but by that time, the pirates had gone, taking their booty with them.

The Boeing 747 could carry up to 550 passengers. From the pirates' point of view, this meant more passengers on more aircraft, physically isolated from the outside world, with no easy chance of escape.

HIJACKING OF THE *PETRO RANGER*

A much more sophisticated attack took place in 1998, when the tanker *Petro Ranger* was hijacked in the South China Sea. This was a major heist. The *Petro Ranger*, which was owned by Petroships of Singapore, was carrying 10,580 tons (9600 tonnes) of diesel fuel and 1764 tons (1600 tonnes) of Jet A1 fuel, together worth some $2.3 million (£4.5 million). The ship was traveling from the Shell Pulau Bukom refinery in Singapore to the oil terminal in Ho Chi Min City in South Vietnam.

The raid had been meticulously planned. Twelve men maneuvered their high-speed motorboats into a blind spot on the *Petro Ranger*'s radar. This allowed them to sweep up unseen, and they climbed onto the ship by means of ropes, grappling hooks, and bamboo ladders. Before the men on watch knew what was happening, they were confronted by pirates, who quickly overpowered them. The pirates sealed off the *Petro Ranger* from outside communications by destroying their satellite, telex, radio, and walkie-talkie equipment.

They then took a hostage and marched him down to the captain's quarters. Meanwhile, the rest of the crew were tied up in the officers' mess, where they remained for 10 days. The pirates proceeded to disguise the ship's identity with the paperwork they had brought with them: fake crew lists, registrations, manifests, cargo details, and a flag of the Central American republic of Honduras, which they ran up the ship's pole. Next, they gave the ship a new name, *Wilby* and with it replaced the name *Petro Ranger* wherever it occurred onboard. The ship's blue funnel was repainted orange.

That done, the pirates set sail for Hainan Island on the southern coast of China near Macau. On the way, two tankers arrived to siphon off the ship's

A panorama of the Greek island of Corfu. There, in 1997, holidaymakers on a hired yacht were attacked and robbed. No ship or boat, however small, seems safe from piracy.

173

Small, lithe Indonesian pirates like those in the picture have the ideal physique for piracy. They climb onboard ship at speed. They move quickly and can make a rapid getaway when a raid is over.

cargo of diesel. But then the whole scheme came apart. Before the ship reached Hainan Island, it was stopped by a Chinese patrol boat. The inspector onboard demanded to see the ship's papers, and soon realized that they were false. The rogue captain and crew were arrested. Afterward, under interrogation, the captain confessed that the attack had been carried out under the orders of an organized crime syndicate based in Singapore, Hong Kong, and Fujian province in China. Had the patrol boat not intervened, the ship would have been used by the syndicate to carry immigrants, illegal arms, or drugs.

The syndicate in question was headed by Chew Cheng Kiat, known in Singapore as David Wong, who operated in the Strait of Malacca in Malaysia and the South China Sea. In 1999, Kiat was found guilty of organizing and financing piracy at a court on the island of Batam in Indonesia and was sentenced to six years' imprisonment.

The *Petro Ranger* was one of the last of Kiat's 22 hijackings. In each case, it transpired that Kiat put a "sleeper" onboard ship disguised as a member of the crew. This man familiarized himself with the ship's accommodation, locating the control rooms and the captain's and officers' quarters, as well as any other information that could be of use to the hijackers when they came aboard. One of the "sleepers" was an Indonesian known as Darman, who took part in the raid on the *Petro Ranger* and worked as second engineer on some four other vessels that were also owned by Petroships.

THE STRAIT OF MALACCA PIRATE HOTSPOT

It is not surprising that in addition to the South China Sea, where the *Petro Ranger* was seized, Chew Chong Kiat was also active in the Strait of Malacca. Of all the waters haunted by modern pirates, the Strait that connects the Indian Ocean with the Pacific Ocean is considered the happiest of hunting grounds. Through this strait, which is some 550 miles (900km) long, passes around one-third of the world's trade each year—three times as much as the Panama Canal and twice as much as the Suez Canal. This includes almost all oil imports for China and Japan. Cargo freighters and oil tankers have proved to be the most favored prey, but all shipping passing through the Strait—up to 60,000 vessels a year—is potentially at risk in a waterway that was the scene of 40 percent of the world's pirate attacks in 2004.

The Strait of Malacca provides an ideal setting for piracy, with its forested shores and small islands furnishing a mass of hiding places from which to launch sudden, unexpected raids on passing traffic. This is particularly true of the Indonesian Riau Islands at the entrance to the Strait of Malacca, which is where the Strait approaches its narrowest point, barely 1.5 miles (2.5km) across.

Some pirates operating in the Strait are opportunists, using small fast boats to make a quick profit by seizing money and valuables, then making off at speed to avoid capture. Gangs of pirates, usually belonging to some crime syndicate (Chew Chong was by no means the only one) are far less spontaneous. They go about their thieving in a carefully organized fashion, armed with sophisticated equipment. They ambush a ship and, once in charge, steal its cargo. The crew is often kidnapped for ransom, or the ship itself is hijacked. This type of pirate attack requires much planning, good funding—and, of course, a certain amount of collusion on the part of the port authorities. In fact, bribing officials to look the other way or accept false papers and manifests as genuine can be a significant expense in piracy.

In addition, countries as well as individuals may be in on the act. Since the 1990s, China has been suspected of supporting pirates in South East Asia and even indulging in piracy on its own account. Since 1995, the possibly nefarious practices of the Chinese Maritime Security Forces in the South China Sea have come to light after complaints from shipowners, crime investigators, and seafarers. It was reported that Chinese patrol boats fired on and boarded merchant ships without good reason. Afterward, several ships that had been classed as "missing" turned up in minor Chinese ports. The local authorities were suspected of seizing the cargoes and selling them off. This, though, was not all. More direct acts of piracy occurred when uniformed soldiers of the Chinese army hijacked ships at sea.

The Chinese government denied everything, although they admitted that some maverick officials "operating illegally" may have been involved. It was also suggested that the Chinese army uniforms could have been a disguise to offload responsibility onto the People's Republic. In 1995, for example, hijackers dressed in these uniforms and, using what appeared to be a Chinese patrol boat, seized a freighter registered in Panama. At the time, the ship was in international waters

The Strait of Malacca provides an ideal setting for piracy, with its forested shores and small islands furnishing a mass of hiding places from which to launch sudden, unexpected raids on passing traffic.

175

en route from Singapore to Cambodia. The hijackers fired shots in the air, presumably as a warning, then boarded the ship and ordered the captain to divert his vessel to Shanwei on the southern coast of China. According to the captain, he and his crew were forced to sign documents professing to be smugglers, then head for China and unload the ship's cargo. The cargo, consisting of cigarettes and photographic equipment worth $2 million (£1,007,500), was taken off the ship by the port authorities. The crew was then allowed to go.

Although the Chinese government refused to accept responsibility for incidents like this, and even, on occasion, tried to shift the blame onto "wicked Westerners," this case proved too controversial. After 1995, Fu Zenghua, assistant director of the Criminal Investigation for China's Public Security Industry announced a tough new policy for dealing with pirates and began a major crackdown. In 1998, the *Cheung Son*, a furnace-slag cargo ship, was hijacked in the South China Sea by pirates posing as customs officials. Afterward, they murdered all 23 members of the crew. Some were stabbed, some shot, and others had their heads covered with bags and were then clubbed to death. The bodies were thrown overboard. By using fishing nets, six of them were later recovered. The ringleader, a corrupt customs official, was arrested together with 49 pirates. Tried in a Chinese court, they were found guilty, and 11 of the pirates were publicly executed by firing squad.

Tried in a Chinese court, they were found guilty, and 11 of the pirates were publicly executed by firing squad.

THE PHILLIP CHANNEL

The narrowest point of the Malacca Strait shipping lane, the Phillip Channel in the Singapore Strait sector, is another waterway where the danger of pirate attack can be acute. Here, the ships' masters need all their skills for several changes of course in order to navigate the narrow waters. In these circumstances, ships must slow down and masters need intense concentration if their ships are going to pass through the Channel safely. Such conditions are an obvious boon to pirates, who usually operate in small groups of up to five men. Avoiding forward-set radar and lookouts on deck, they sidle up to the stern of a ship in a *prahu* (a native skiff up to 10ft/3m long), throw up grappling hooks, and climb onto the deck. One of their first tasks is to cut a mooring rope and then hang the sliced end over the stern as an escape route when their work is finished.

Most of these pirates are Indonesians. Their slight but lithe physique makes them ideal for the task of getting onto and off of a ship at speed and sometimes in silence. Their dark skin provides them with natural camouflage, because most attacks take place at night. Many raids occur without a ship's crew even realizing it until the pirates have gone, leaving only plundered safes and ransacked cabins. More often, though, the presence of pirates onboard is not known until they actually appear on deck. An entire raid may take only six minutes as the pirates put machetes or knives to the throats of one of the officers or the ship's helmsman to force the captain to go down to his cabin and open his safe. Between 1981 and 1983 alone, a total of 51 of these quick hit-and-run attacks occurred on ships in the Phillip Channel.

The Malacca Strait, however, has several rivals in the Philippines and elsewhere for the dubious accolade of the world's most dangerous waterway. In the Philippines, for example, 1983 witnessed up to 122 robberies in just one of its ports, General Santos in the south of Mindanao island. In West Africa,

where Nigeria suffers from encroaching desert, increasing population, and poor farmland, poverty is endemic. Consequently, so too is piracy. From the 1980s onward, ships waiting for berths in Nigerian ports, sometimes far out to sea, became easy and frequent targets for pirate attacks. Security was so lax at times that gangs of around 50 pirates touting knives and sometimes firearms roamed the decks without anyone trying to stop or even challenge them. They received a certain amount of help from officials who were either bribed or threatened into colluding with the pirates. Specific cargo was sometimes targeted, suggesting that someone had previously "leaked" information about what was in a ship's hold. Police who were supposed to ensure safety onboard ship were mysteriously

These Malaysian police have a difficult job to do in the Malacca Straits, one of the most dangerous waterways in the world and one that is constantly infested by pirates.

January 20, 2006: A team from the guided missile destroyer *Winston S. Churchill* is shown heading for a suspected pirate ship off the Malaysian coast with a view to boarding and inspecting it.

absent when a pirate attack was under way. Police launches would keep their distance, even though a ship was encircled by a pack of pirate canoes. Even more suspicious were the activities of the so-called "bow-and-arrow" men, who were hired as guards but were much more likely to be in league with the pirates. So were crooked shipping agents or port officials in places like Brazil. In some Brazilian ports, prior knowledge of a ship's cargo became evident when pirates ignored the lesser prizes and headed for the more valuable cargo—usually high-tech equipment.

Yet another method used by pirates was to exploit the window of opportunity offered when crews were fully occupied berthing the ship while security staff waited to come onboard. Some pirates realized that this was the time to sneak onto a ship, grab whatever booty was most easily to handle, and slip away uncaught and frequently unseen. Abuses like these were so common that shipping companies and cargo owners made frequent complaints to international bodies, including the European Union and various seafarers' organizations, insisting that something must be done, and quickly. In 1981, Nigeria responded by forming a combined-service harbor patrol force and banning canoes with outboard motors (the pirates' getaway vehicles) from coming anywhere near their ports. In addition, Nigeria promised a coast guard to monitor its territorial waters. At first, the new rules seemed to work. Pirate attacks dropped dramatically from 72 between March and December 1981 to a mere six in the following nine months. These reduced further in 1984, when only one attack by pirates occurred in Nigerian waters.

NEW FORMS OF ATTACK AND RESPONSE

Such improvements in piracy control, though impressive, were only temporary because the precautions of the 1980s did not remain sufficient for long. Increasingly, as time went on, it was not enough for crews to defend themselves using searchlights or Aldis lamps to scan the surrounding waters, or to release gas bombs to frighten off pirates. Other measures became just as outdated and ineffective with time, such as the duty officer being given two or more watchmen to continuously patrol the deck. And rather than slowing to a stop while a ship waited for a pilot to steer her into port, captains soon realized that it was safer for the ship to keep on cruising to prevent pirates from exploiting this opportunity to come aboard themselves. Such precautions did not become useless. Rather, after a very few years, they failed to cope with the ever-increasing sophistication of pirate tactics and weaponry.

Like war, piracy has long been a contest between new forms of attack and, in response, new forms of defense or strategies. When confronted by a heavily armed defense, pirates simply adopt even more destructive weapons, such as more powerful handguns and machine-guns or rocket-propelled grenades. And when thwarted in one of their hunting grounds, for instance, pirates move to another. Since most of the world's seas, apart from European and North American waters, are susceptible to piracy, there is plenty of alternative space for pirates to infest.

The pirates' response to official efforts designed to curb their activities will also be influenced by the amount of wealth at their disposal. Pirates hunting for prey in the Arabian Sea can afford to use anti-tank missiles, whereas less well funded West African pirates have to make do in a more primitive fashion, with knives and canoes launched from fishing boats.

In this context, poverty and piracy inevitably go together. In an age when survival still remains a struggle for most of the world's inhabitants and a struggle lost by millions, thieving and piracy will—and does—replace honest toil. Certainly, there is very little sign that poverty has significantly lessened in Africa or anywhere else where piracy is still rife over the decades since World War II. Neither has corruption, which Robert Walpole (1676–1745), Britain's first prime minister, once called "the natural state of human affairs." Where pirates or the

Increasingly, as time went on, it was not enough for crews to defend themselves by using searchlights or Aldis lamps to scan the surrounding waters or release gas bombs to frighten off pirates.

UNFETTERED PIRACY
At one Nigerian port, named Apapa, near Lagos, and also at ports in Sierra Leone and Ghana, security was so lax that gangs of thieves simply sauntered up and down the wharf, waiting to steal cargoes as soon as they were landed. Other pirates had the nerve to go onboard ships berthed by the quayside and throw cargo over the side: below, men were waiting in canoes to catch and stow the booty and afterward make off at speed.

crime syndicates that back some of them can bribe or threaten the police or judiciary into doing what they want, there is not much room for law and order and great danger for companies or individuals attempting to fight back.

MORE EXPEDIENT TO STAY SILENT THAN FIGHT BACK

There is also a curious situation in which the safeguards against piracy offered by governments and other interested organizations are resisted by the victims themselves. Where crews, or even entire ships and their cargoes, have been taken for ransom, it seems that shipowners would rather pay up than wait in port at a cost of up to $10,000 (£5000) a day, while officials conduct lengthy investigations into the crime. Another problem is that ships hijacked by pirates acquire a bad reputation, which neither its owners, captain, and crew are willing to encourage. A more practical reason for avoiding legal proceedings is the fear that a ship's insurers will increase premiums once a vessel has been hijacked. According to

The so-called Vietnamese Boat People, who were persistently hounded at sea by pirates, were tragic refugees fleeing from home in the aftermath of the Vietnam war, which ended in 1975.

Mohamed Said Barre was president of Somalia from 1969 to 1991, when he was overthrown by rebels. Before he came to power, Barre served in the police and army and politically was inclined toward Marxism.

the International Maritime Organization, such considerations help account for the fact that around one-half of pirate attacks go unreported.

Victims of piracy are also reluctant to risk going to court because of the widespread links between piracy and syndicates of organized crime, with their well-known penchant for getting their way by extreme violence. In the Pacific, where piracy has been rife for many years, there seems to be little chance of escaping the tentacles of crime syndicates whose power encompasses almost the entire ocean. The southern area of the South China Sea and the Malacca Strait is controlled by the Singapore syndicate. Thailand, Mayanmar (formerly Burma) and Malaysia, which border the Andaman Sea are covered from Bangkok, and the

Chinese triads in Hong Kong hold sway over the northern area of the South China Sea. Jakarta, Indonesia's capital, covers the fourth sector, the Java Sea and parts of the South China Sea up to the coast of Borneo.

Between them, these crime syndicates run branches in Cambodia, mainland China, Malaysia, Mayanmar, the Philippine Islands, Sumatra, and Vietnam. Any vessel targeted by the syndicates therefore moves from one controlled area to the next with little chance of avoiding a hijack somewhere along the way. The most susceptible are those carrying goods or materials that can be sold on the black market, such as kerosene and diesel fuel, refined palm oil, copper, aluminum, copper, and steel. The pirate gangs sent out by the syndicates to harvest these riches are not poverty-stricken desperadoes but well-organized professional operatives. The syndicates often run legitimate businesses as covers for their illegal activities, which include drug running, stealing cargoes, and smuggling immigrants, as well as capturing and ransacking ships.

Political upheavals, too, provide a way in for piracy. Instability causes law and order to collapse, whole populations are displaced, and virtually every crime it is possible to commit stalks everyday life. One such instance was provided by the Vietnam war of 1959–75, where an outbreak of piracy followed the final withdrawal of American troops. Most victims were Vietnamese "boat people" seeking political asylum and willing to face extreme conditions at sea in fragile craft. Unfortunately, the dangers included attacks by pirates, often Thais operating in the South China Sea, who robbed, raped, terrorized, and, not infrequently, murdered the refugees.

Similarly Somalia, on the Horn of Africa, has become a focus of piracy since 1991, when local warlords ousted Mohamed Said Barre (1919–95), an army colonel who had seized power over 20 years before. What followed the collapse of central government in Somalia was a reign of terror fronted by local warlords with the connivance of Al Qaeda terrorists, and an outbreak of aggressive piracy at sea. Heavily armed men touting automatic rifles and rocket-propelled grenades began to prowl Somali waters in fishing boats, seeking prey. Hijackings became so frequent that the International Maritime Bureau (IMB) based in London issued warnings to ships to avoid the Somali coast, where 37 pirate attacks were recorded in a single year, 2005/06. In the seven months between March and August 2005 alone, 15 attacks took place, compared with just two in the whole of 2004. One group of pirates involved, known as the Somali Marines, used a large

The syndicates often run legitimate businesses as covers for their illegal activities, which include drug running, stealing cargoes, and smuggling immigrants, as well as capturing and ransacking ships.

STEALING FROM STARVING SOMALIA

Pirates are not always fussy about what they steal. Some ships attacked in recent years were carrying food aid desperately needed in Somalia. Civil war, famine, drought, floods, storms, an Ethiopian invasion in 2006, and the ruinous tsunami at the end of the same year, created a serious humanitarian crisis in which two million Somalis were said to be starving. In addition, pirates who kidnapped for ransom did so with such frequency that they created a tariff for the crime, setting the price for releasing a victim at $500,000 (£250,000) per head.

"mother ship" to launch attacks on shipping from small boats by a few men armed with machine-guns and rocket-propelled grenades.

A crewman on the pirate skiff off the Somali coast in March 2006 looks down at the sea while still in international waters. Not long afterward, the skiff was attacked and totally consumed by flames.

THE STRUGGLE AGAINST PIRACY

Today, almost 30 years after Nigeria was pressurized into implementing rules to counteract piracy in her own coastal waters, the search is still on for more effective ways to eliminate the problem. This is truly a global war, being fought along the eastern and western coasts of Africa, in South America, Bangladesh, India, and parts of the Caribbean. Everywhere, pirates use inflatables and fishing boats with souped-up engines. They target anything that floats, from yachts, bulk carriers, and large freighters, to general cargo ships, luxury cruise liners, and even tankers. They steal anything and everything that is not bolted down.

The struggle to counteract piracy has come a long way since the 1980s and now features a good deal of international co-operation. In 2006, two of the countries whose shipping is most at risk from piracy, Singapore and Indonesia, launched regular sea and air patrols intended to spot pirate vessels while they are still some distance from their prey. Additionally, the FASA (Federation of Asian Shipowners' Associations) has created a database that offers information on the location of pirate attacks, their type, and their outcome. This is matched by a system pioneered by the Information Sharing Center, in which 14 countries have joined together to thwart piracy in Asia. India joined in 2006. The Strait of

Today, the coast of Somalia is infested with pirates. But this pirate skiff, shown consumed by flames and burgeoning smoke in international waters in March 2006, was not one of the successful raiders.

Malacca, so dangerous for any shipping, is currently patrolled by a multinational anti-pirate force.

A UAV (unmanned aerial vehicle) patrol base is being constructed by India in the Andaman and Nicobar Islands to monitor the Andaman Sea, which lies close to the Strait. The UAVs are usually fixed-wing aircraft, but sometimes rotorcraft can also be useful spy-in-the-sky devices. Among their remote-sensing functions, electromagnetic sensors include infrared or near infrared cameras that, together with their radar systems, are able to detect and record the approach of pirate vessels. UAVs may be remotely controlled or follow flights that have been previously programmed into their software. Another sophisticated high-tech device is known as Shiploc. This can be installed on ships, and carries a long-range satellite tracking and identification system. It operates round the clock, monitoring the location of ships, their speed, and their heading.

Onboard ship, protection against pirates may be provided by highly trained security personnel, constant vigilance, and all the ingenuity that high-tech can provide. For a start, some of the toughest men in the world, the sort that no pirate would like to meet on one of the dark nights when they normally operate, have been hired as security guards by shipping and cruise-liner companies. These men mean business. Among them are recruits from Britain's Royal Navy and Royal Marines, one-time commandos from the Israeli Defense Force, and the famous Gurkhas of Nepal, who have proved their courage, enterprise—and ruthlessness—ever since they first fought alongside the British Army in 1817.

HIGH- AND LOW-TECH BOTH PLAY A ROLE
Shipboard defenses today are meant to stop short of killing pirates. The intention is simply to disable them, because a dead pirate is not nearly as useful as a live

These Somali marines belong to the most powerful group of pirates operating along the African coast. Their base area is the coast of Somalia, where they deal in drugs and weapons, and smuggle humans.

On November 5, 2005, the US cruise ship *Seabourne Spirit*, seen here having its flank painted, was attacked by Somali pirates, who left an unexploded grenade on board. It was removed by bomb experts.

captive, who can be interrogated for information about the criminal bosses behind their raids or future activities being planned. In the twenty-first century, technology has reached a higher degree of sophistication than ever before, although simpler technology still has its part to play. For example, barbed wire running along the ship's railings is a simple, low-tech device that prevents pirates getting onto the deck of a ship. A more vicious version of the same idea is a 9000-volt electrical fence that makes the deck even less easy to reach when extended outward from the ship's exterior. On some ships, the fence has additionally been fitted with radar to give warning of approaching vessels. Motion sensors are another useful item because they can detect pirates while

they are boarding the ship otherwise unseen. Ships' bridges fitted with cameras and voice recorders also help identify pirates.

Similarly, fire hoses powerful enough to wash pirates off the deck and into the sea have been installed on some ships. Stun grenades and pepper sprays can also be used to put pirates out of action long enough to enable their capture. The Long-Range Acoustic Device (LRAD), better known as a sonic cannon or more graphically "the parabolic audio boom-box," is a truly disconcerting weapon. It sends out a deafeningly loud noise that no human ear can stand for long. When turned on, pirates have been known to jump into the sea to escape it. In 2005, off the coast of East Africa, the luxury cruise liner *Seabourne Spirit* was approached by two speedboats that fired a rocket-propelled grenade and machine-guns at her. To make the pirates reconsider their actions, the ship's chief of security used a sonic cannon, supported by electronic simulators that gave the pirates the impression the ship was firing back at them. Foams and glues can also be sprayed on the decks, making it impossible for pirates to stay upright, while low-frequency sound waves will induce bowel movements.

BOOTY IN BILLIONS LOST TO PIRACY

Yet despite these deterrents, whether low- or high-tech, ingenious or simple, it has been estimated that booty amounting to $18 billion (£9 billion) is still being lost to piracy every year. In 2006, more than 209 pirate attacks were reported worldwide, together with 77 crewmen kidnapped and 188 taken hostage. Of these attacks, 15 ended in murder. Attacks in 2006 were some 24 percent down on the 276 recorded for 2005. At the time, this was greeted as "encouraging," but piracy statistics tend to fluctuate and only a year later, in 2007, attacks were on the way up again, rising by 25 percent to 263. Moreover, attacks involving the use of guns increased by 35 percent. Meanwhile, Indonesia, with the Strait of Malacca on its doorstep and scores of its 17,000 islands ideal for use as pirate haunts, remained the most frequent venue for piracy, and 37 pirate raids took place there in the first 10 months of 2007.

Nor has the impudence of some pirate attacks lessened. On January 23, 2005, a bulk carrier was in port at Balikpapan, on the Indonesian island of Borneo, when 10 pirates came aboard, armed with knives. They assaulted the duty officer, tied him up, and proceeded to steal property and then escaped by climbing down the anchor chain. This was not some clandestine operation. Cargo was unloaded while the raid was going on: stevedores were on board, moving the cargo onto barges drawn up alongside both sides of the ship. So was an armed policeman. Nevertheless, the raiders seem to have been undetected and got clean away.

More than 3300 years have passed since piracy first made Earth's oceans, seas, and waterways dangerous. Now and again, pirates have been controlled: when the Romans gained the upper hand in ancient times; when the Shogun Iemitsu severed Japan from the outside world, and the wokou pirates with it; and when Europeans cracked down hard on piracy to preserve their overseas empires. But all the while piracy has persisted, even if it was low key, waiting to emerge again when the power of their erstwhile opponents declined and passed into history. And in spite of what sophisticated technology can do and however hard the fight to suppress it, piracy still infests the waters of the world. Pirates have not finished with us yet.

Foams and glues can be sprayed on the decks, making it impossible for pirates to stay upright, while low-frequency sound waves will induce bowel movements.

BIBLIOGRAPHY

Burnett, John S. *Dangerous Waters: Modern Piracy and Terror on the High Seas* (Plume, Penguin Group, UK 2003)

Exquemelin, Alexander O. *The Buccaneers of America* (Dover Publications Inc., Mineola, New York, USA 1969)

Gosse, Philip. *The History of Piracy* (Originally published 1932. Dover Publications Inc., Mineola, New York, USA 2007)

Keble Chatterton, E. *Pirates and Piracy* (Originally published 1914. Dover Publications Inc., Mineola, New York, USA 2006)

Lucie–Smith, Edward. *Outcasts of the Sea: Pirates and Piracy* (Paddington Press, UK 1978)

O'Donnell, Liam. *The Pirate Code* (Edge Books, Capstone Press, Mankato, Minnesota, USA 2007)

Ormerod, Henry A. *Piracy in the Ancient World* (Originally published 1924. The Johns Hopkins University Press, Baltimore, Maryland, USA 1997)

Sherry, Frank. *Raiders and Rebels: The Golden Age of Piracy* (Hearst Maritime Books, New York, USA 1986)

Turnbull, Stephen. *Pirate of the Far East* (Osprey Publishing, UK 2007)

Villar, Captain Roger. *Piracy Today: Robbery and Violence at Sea Since 1980* (Conway Maritime Press, UK 1985)

INDEX

PICTURE CREDITS

Bridgeman Art Library: 6/7, 19 (Bibliotheque Nationale), 26, 28 (Giraudon), 35, 41 (Peter Newark Historical Pictures), 42 (Prado), 43, 46 (Peter Newark Pictures), 48 (Archives Charmet), 49 (Peter Newark Historical Pictures), 50 (Ken Welsh), 57 (Calmann & King), 61 (National Trust Photographic Library), 67 (Giraudon), 68 (National Palace Museum), 70, 89 (Peter Newark Historical Pictures), 90, 92 (Peter Newark Pictures), 95, 105 (Giraudon), 107 (Stapleton Collection), 108, 109 (Peter Newark American Pictures), 114, 117 & 118 (Peter Newark Historical Pictures), 123 (Musee de la Marine), 127 & 129 (Peter Newark Pictures), 133, 135 (Crown Estate), 136 (Library of Congress), 139 (Peter Newark Historical Pictures), 140 (Look & Learn), 141 (Library of Congress), 146 (Look & Learn), 148, 149 (Peter Newark Historical Pictures), 153, 158 (Peter Newark Pictures), 161 & 162 (Peter Newark Pictures), 164

Cody Images: 180 (US Navy)

Corbis: 10/11 (Vanni Archive), 54/55, 56 (Steven Vidler), 58 (Asian Art & Archaeology), 63 (Christie's Images), 71 (Asian Art & Archaeology), 76/77 (Bettmann), 78, 81 (Mariners' Museum), 83 & 97 (Bettmann), 102 (Bettmann), 157, 166/167 (Supri/Reuters), 173 (James Davis), 174 (Crack Palinggi/Reuters), 181 (Henri Bureau/Sygma)

De Agostini Picture Library: 13, 17 (D. Dagli Orti), 20 (G. Cozzi), 29, 64

Getty Images: 98/99 & 111 (Hulton Archive), 185 & 186 (AFP)

Heritage Image Partnership: 34 & 40 (The Print Collector)

iStockphoto: 88t (Valerie Loiseleux), 88b (Christine Balderas)

Mary Evans Picture Library: 12, 16, 21, 22, 25, 31, 32/33, 37 (ILN Pictures), 39, 44, 47, 53 (Rue Des Archives), 62, 65, 72, 75, 80, 84, 87, 94 (Grosvenor Prints), 100, 113, 120/121, 122, 124, 125, 126, 128, 134, 143, 144/145, 150, 152, 154, 165, 169

Photos.com: 14, 82, 116, 155

Photos12.com: 103 (Collection Cinéma), 130 (Ann Ronan Picture Library)

Rex Features: 170 & 177 (Sipa Press), 183 & 184 (Sipa Press)

US Department of Defense: 178 (US Navy)